THE M

Albert Morris: "Standing brooding on life, at my favourite bus stop in dear grey-rain-and-wind grieved, catarrhal Edinburgh."

THE
MORRIS FILE

A collection of works by

ALBERT MORRIS

illustrations by Stewart MacGregor

THE SCOTSMAN
and
G.R.F. SUTHERLAND & Co.

ISBN 0 902670 02 6

Originally published in book form 1985

by The Scotsman, 20 North Bridge, Edinburgh
and
G.R.F. Sutherland & Co.

Typeset by Waverley Graphics Ltd., Edinburgh.
Printed by Ivanhoe Printing Co. Ltd., Musselburgh.

Contents

Foreword

FROM time to editorial time, readers have suggested that selections from my columnar writing ought to be printed in book form. To them I replied that one day, possibly when the fields were white with imaginative daisies or in some season of mental mists and mellow literary fruitfulness, I would buckle down to the task and try to get a sample of my journalistic goods between unplain covers so that they could be appreciated by a discerning public or at least deplored en masse.

When Mr George Sutherland, managing director of the Ivanhoe Printing Company Ltd of Musselburgh invited me to lunch and between the soup and the fish suggested that some of my daily effusions could be made into a book, I paled beneath my light Edinburgh tan.

While the suggestion was flattering—and I am not the man to turn down the odd copper or two in royalties—sudden dread seized my troubled mind. It was not so much the attendant problems of publishing the book, such as the world television, film and broadcasting rights and the fact that some of the less active members of the public might get knocked down in the rush to buy copies, but a realisation that, being of a lighthearted and whimsical turn of mind, I had promised a few readers—say about 5,000—who had, over the years asked me when such a book would be published, that I would, if the happy event occurred, send them free, signed copies.

If you will take the word of a gentleman ranker, late of His Majesty's Army, that was said just in fun; only to raise the hint of a ghost of a smile. Would you all bankrupt me for a jest?

I know I can trust my readers to play the straight bat, pay up and look, as Samuel Pepys said about the hanging, drawing and quartering of one Major-General Harrison, "as cheerful as any man could in that condition."

Readers, I must say vary—sometimes sharply—in their reaction to my writing. Some would have me horsewhipped or treated in the manner of that unfortunate officer, while others believed that there is no better writer for helping them to get through their high-fibre, low-interest breakfast at a brisk, crackling pace or putting them to sleep at night as if felled with a mace. Most, however, are extremely kind and their letters are often a great source of encouragement to me.

Once, in my ardent manhood, a girl to whom I had spoken at length on the agricultural production statistics of southern Slovenia, said: "Albert Morris, you must know just about everything." Surely the child was deceived but I must reveal that to run such a vast columnar complex, with its massive tautology reduction plant, its huge Blohm and Voss, triple-expansion, flat-bed printing works, to say nothing of its prose-purpling and verb-deactivation complexes, requires a particularly wide general knowledge.

I do not claim to posses that entirely and I must reveal that rich sources of information come especially from the always-helpful staff of "The Scotsman" library and also from other members of the paper's well-informed editorial staff.

People have asked me where I get my ideas from for the column. They come from newspapers, magazines and other journals, from personal experiences, from readers and from standing, brooding on life, at my favourite bus stop in dear, grey-rain-and-wind-grieved, catarrhal Edinburgh.

Sometimes, they occur to me of a sleepless night but often in the middle of a good meal, during which I may lavishly entertain an idea, claiming, of course, the money in legitimate expenses.

The selections have been taken from as far back as the mid-seventies with the exception of the article about teaching my mother to play chess, which was a pre-columnar piece, and included in memory of my parent who was often an inadvertent inspiration for my writing.

I would like to thank all connected with the preparation of this book, including Mr Eric Mackay, the former editor of "The Scotsman", hard working secretaries, colleague Stewart MacGregor who drew the illustrations, sub-editors who handled my work over the years, often above and beyond the call of normal editorial duty, and of course, the redoubtable and dependable Miss Angela Primstone, chatelaine of the columnar wine cupboard who urges me onto my daily tasks with spirited words and gestures and who, if she did not exist, would have to be invented.

Lastly, my anticipatory thanks to any who buy the book. Remember, it can also be used as a draught excluder, a door-jam, an effective fly-swatter and, if several copies are placed on the head, a posture improver.

If you just want to read it in bookshops, please don't turn down the pages. Assistants—and I write from experience—are apt to get edgy.

1

Knot for my comfort

AS I walk about mine own city—here—helping old ladies across the street despite occasional protests that they do not want to go; there, deliberately ignoring youths with grass-green hair, mud-coloured minds, pink eyes and purple lips who seem to think they ought to be the focus of all wondering eyes and sometimes raising my hat to lady traffic wardens who stare at me narrowly as if I were suspected of placing beer-can rings in meters—I note how the compost heap of my memory has grown from the days when it was mere molehill, with hardly a recollection pebble on it, to something that now resembles a wind-grieved peak in the Himalayas.

Here I see a building that once contained a shop that sold me ranks of grim-faced model soldiers who could fight and run away and live to fight another day, and which has now been taken over by a shop containing grim-faced assistants specialising in a surrealistic display of cast-off consumer durables.

Somewhere else I will see a lamp-post—or at least the concrete successor to the old gas one—around which I twirled myself as a child in a curious game that many of my peer group played which spun our consciousness into new unstable dimensions and for moments made us feel that we had reached some Nirvana in which we stood still and the earth, the solar system and the known universe itself, whirled madly round us.

11

There, yes there, is the school, now showing signs of maintenance neglect in which I thought the thoughts of youth and heard the words: Albert Morris, you are a stumer," that one by one, by and large, and in a manner of speaking, the touch of life has turned to truth.

Round the corner, past the side street in which I, a conkering hero, flicked my adamintine horse chestnut to stringed victory in battles against the brittle offerings of foes, stands the old church hall in which I functioned once a week as a Wolf Cub, dyb-dyb-dobbing, knot-tying, learning all about animal spoors in the African and Indian bush and imbiding mentally large, nutritious, chunks of *The Jungle Book,* by Mr Kipling who clung to the—for us cubs—somewhat mystifying philosophy that East was East and West was West and never the twain would meet until certain extraordinary conditions were fulfilled.

At least the church hall stood, albeit in the last stages of decrepitude and decay, until the other day. Now, it had gone, shattered by the fell hand of demolishers and in its place stood an empty space, rubbled and sterile as a portion of lunar landscape.

If I had worn a hat, I would have raised it then in silent salute to the old place in which I learned about the law of the jungle from the Mowgli stories and which seemed designed to make impressionable youths fit to tackle life in a laissez-faire capitalist society, how to tell where North was by the use of a watch only and the merest glimpse of sun and to tie a variety of knots which not only were useful in mooring craft from yachts to ocean liners, carrying barrels of rum or other liquids on board ships and joining two pieces of rope together but were in themselves examples of tenacious, unslippable, qualities which our cub mistresses said British

boys ought to develop to hold the Empire together in a nice, neat and tidy, red-coloured parcel.

Akela was my knot mentor. Standing beside the broken bricks, shattered stone and mud that marked what remained of the hall, I could still see her, the evening sun shining through the stained-glass windows and giving her the look of some damsel painted by one of the pre-Raphaelite school.

Ah, that perfect 17-year-old profile, the freshly-ironed neckerchief that spoke of purity, integrity and a knowledge of knots, that authoritative woggle. How, we grubby cubs, many of us, for enlightened reasons, generally covered in mire and washing only, if we could get away with it, on alternate Thursdays, were staggered by our first real sight of female beauty. Shirley Temple in all her tap-dancing, curly haired glory had nothing on her. Could the child star tie a sheep-bend? Her pictures gave no indication of that and we assumed the worst.

Of course, there were other female assistants about Aleka, all bearing the names of animal characters in *The Jungle Book*, but although they were fine specimens of healthy, muscular, bright-eyed, Scottish girlhood, they were meaner beauties of the skies who paled into insignificance when the moon of Akela rose to initiate us into the mysteries of the bowline knot.

"This," said Akela holding up a piece of demonstrational cord, "is how you tie the bowline. What is it called Albert?" "A bowline miss," I answered with the terrible promptness of childhood, and a blush of pleasure would suffuse the delicate features of the girl as she knew her lesson was sinking home.

How I remember it all. The rabbit hole formed by one end of the cord, the other end being the rabbit that went round and darted down the hole, thence to form "a knot that will not slip," said Akela who hinted that it was essentially a British knot, as unremovable as a British square against the dancing Dervishes.

Of course, it was not all knots. Sometimes, we gathered round Akela and her acolytes and sang songs about ten green bottles hanging on the wall, the symbolic significance of which has now escaped me, that we would never go to heaven in a rocking chair and that we were "Itch Ae P P Wy." We also recited the cub promise that we would be clean in thought, word and deed, if not actually in body, help others as we meant to help ourselves and keep the law of the wolf cub pack even though we were the last survivor of a beleagured garrison with the wily Pathans crawling up for a social introduction or if we were arthritically playing football in the courtyard of an old folks' home.

Occasionally Akela's face would become troubled as she realised her terrible responsibilities of moulding young male minds. Then she would take a deep breath, shoulder her task, face the issue spuarely, and tell us certain facts of life as she knew them.

"Moss," she disclosed on one particularly solemn occasion—and was there a modest maidenly blush on her damask cheeks as she spoke?—"invariably grows on the north side of trees, lightning seldom strikes the same place twice and if you find yourselves in India's sunny clime or in the burning sands of Africa, remember to boil your drinking water and wear your solar topee all the time."

I used to follow her spoor when she left the hall at the end of the pack meeting so that I could protect her from any danger, not so much by imposing my body between her and it, but by shouting in a childish treble, very loudly, and running off in search of the characteristics footprints of some long, loping constable.

Fortunately that never happened but had it done so I am certain I would have been worthy of my woggle.

Akela's training is, of course, still with me and I try to pass it on to young Britons. The other day I stopped a young office typist in her tracks and asked if she would like to learn the bowline knot. "No thank you," she said curtly and made off at high speed, about 240 leg movements a minute.

Never mind, Akela, I'll still go on trying to impart your knowledge. A former British bowline boy has turned into an unslipping watchdog of the public weal. The old hall may be gone but by the big brown bear Balloo and the whiskers of Bagheera, I'm still dob, dob, dobbing along.

2

Sand in my prose

I was in a cheerful mood and inclined to let the office know about it. "Primmers," I shouted in my male chauvinistic way that has made me so beloved by all right-thinking females, "fetch aft the morning coffee and look sharp about it."

Miss Angela Primstone, chatelaine of the columnar wine cupboard, a dignified procession of one, glided into the room as if on castors, with a steaming cup of a little-known Albanian blend, much favoured by the more progressive intellectuals in this office. Her honest face showed undisguised pleasure at hearing her name so affectionately shortened by the young master.

In fact what I had to tell her instantly removed the smile from her features and replaced it with a look of dismay, disappointment and distress as well as a suspicion of two crystalline tear-drops forming at the corners of her deep-set hazel eyes.

"I may be departing this office and our Socialist paradise for good, Miss Primstone" I said.

"I have in fact along with a Mr Don Revie—whoever and whatever he may be and frankly I don't care—received an offer of a five-year contract worth £500,000 tax-free, not including service charge, to go out to the Middle East and do, for its humour what Revie will no doubt do for the football of the United Arab Emirates team."

For some time my office has been the scene of hush-hush, behind-closed-doors, top-secret talks with many refined

17

Arab dignitaries from certain sheikh-doms who have been represented by a Mr Mustapha Bakhandah. Not only would I be asked to organise a team of fast-talking, hard-writing, no-punch-pulling columnists in these humorously-underdeveloped countries, but I would also be solely responsible for the production of crude humour and unrefined jokes, in the western part of the Persian Gulf to a distance of 18 miles out to sea, ships of foreign nationality not included.

Apart from the money, I would be given a magnificent, air-cooled, 24-roomed house—the former seraglio palace of a deposed Sultan—with grave, silently-moving servants, dancing girls with or without yashmaks, bearing sherbert and themselves with dignity.

The minute I saw the flowing robes of Mr Bakhandah and observed his gold teeth flash like battle blades in the sun, I knew that here was someone with whom any reasonable person—let alone myself—could deal. I had to confess that I liked the affectionate way he flicked the currency notes of the Gulf state of El Katarrh under my nose, each newly-printed in consecutive numbers and showing a portrait of the Emir Rumh el Baba scowling at a traditional Arab missile system in the middle distance. I was also touched by the way he kept slipping mint Maria Theresa dollars into my palm when my attention was distracted. I felt that he was trying to tell me something and on inquiry found that that was indeed the case.

Humour in the Persian Gulf, he told me, was poor, friable stuff, apt to crumble on the tongue when uttered in the presence of the police or internal security chief. Experts however had shown that proven reserves of rich jocular veins were only waiting to be tapped by someone like myself, skilled in western joke technology.

What was needed, Mr Bakhandah claimed, was someone—he mentioned no names but looked me fully in the face with half-averted eyes—prepared to sweat it out for a few rewarding years, getting sand in my prose and balance in my bank statement while Britain was denuded of my presence—and serve it right for being so ungrateful, he said with a laugh that sounded like an oil slick pleasantly slithering on the shore.

In the Gulf, I would be expected to have constructed a vast complex of crude humour refineries, including giant joke crackers, verbiage separators and meaning extractors as well as single and double entendre production lines. The complex would turn out high-grade, general-purpose, heavy-duty humour that would after a time put the Persian Gulf on the world's jocular map from where it had been omitted for too long.

At present the area had only three stock jokes, the one about the caliph and the one-legged water carrier having been in existence, it is estimated from carbon-dating and other methods, from about the time of Alexander the Great.

The origin and date of another—about why the camel crossed the sand dune—is also lost in the mists of Jocular antiquity, but a suggestion from the British Museum that it originated in Ur of the Chaldees cannot be totally ignored.

The third, an obscure one about the wooden-legged inside-right of a harem football team, is in general use with local variations in plot, although its construction is said to be as rickety as a water-clock.

I saw Miss Primstone plying her handkerchief vigorously at my news and patted her reassuringly in the shoulder. "There, there," I said. "If you will wait a few months I might be able to send out for you and together we could spark a flame of humour that might spread like wildfire across the burning sands and beyond." Miss Primstone dried her eyes. "I will wait forever if need be, Mr Morris," she said simply but effectively.

What, I asked her, was there left for me in Britain? Nothing but repining letters from "Disgusted Mother of Five, Scunthorpe," and "Paterfamilias, Hankow," as well as continual telegrams and phone calls stating that I should be horse-whipped to within a millimetre of my miserable life.

"It's disheartening, all this criticism, Miss Primstone," I said. "I'm a very sensitive person, you know. I am certain that the Arabs would take a very different view of my literary efforts and spur me on with word, gesture and wildly-extravagant payments."

Yesterday Mr Bakhandah brought in the contract for signing and as I unscrewed my fountain pen (that would cost the Arabs 15 guineas for a start) and hovered over the dotted line, Mr Bakhandah regaled me with stories about how previous humorists who had come out from Britain, Cuba, and the USSR to develop the area's potential and bring it within their own country's sphere of humour influence had been boiled in oil if they failed to bring a smile to the Rumh el Baba's knife-pared features.

I turned on my hells and left, the contract unsigned. Somehow I had changed my mind. "Primmers," I shouted, "fetch aft the claret and seed cake. I'm going to stay in Britain and fight until the last joke." Miss Primstone's face lit up like a turnip lantern. Someone appreciated me here. I was content.

The Arabs would just have to make the best of what humour they had. Just let them laugh that off.

3

Sour puss

WANTED: Cat, pure in thought, word and deed, educated up to the feline equivalent of five A levels. Colour—immaterial but must be able to match furniture, fittings and general landscape in home of quiet suburban family of fair-to-average tastes and with no axe to grind. Shifts: flexi-time encouraged, plenty of opportunity for recreational activities. Successful candidate will be politically centrist, ecology conscious, classical music lover and be willing to share household diet ranging from supreme de volaille Maryland to occasional sardines from the tin. Must be good mouser, watchdog, as well as guide, friend and philosopher. Applications will be treated strictly in confidence.

I had thought of putting this advertisement in the journals that exist to further the interest of felines and their owners in this cat-crowded isle because getting an educated and articulate cat was proving more difficult than my wife and I had thought.

After a week's interviewing, now rejecting one animal—a Persian who looked as if it would have shown only affection only for the late Shah and no-one else—and turning down others because they did not go with the carpets and curtains—"what you want," said a cat expert, "is one that will not go for the carpets and curtains"—we felt ourselves wondering whether a small, not-too-demanding, tortoise might not fit the ambience of our household and turn itself into an occasionally-moving tasteful ornament.

21

We did not feel we were asking for much in the way of a cat because most of the owners we know seem to have felines that apparently combine the brains of a Leonardo da Vinci with one of the shrewder international merchant bankers.

We wanted a cat only with the aforesaid qualifications plus a refined speaking voice and a certain brisk ability in dealing with other cat intruders in the Morris domain. Not much really but you would have thought we were asking for the moon plus several planets the way some owners who had cats for sale or disposal, reacted.

"This is just your ordinary Moggie," one woman said, holding up a badly-stuffed puss that regarded us with an expression of extreme distaste. "Basic model, no trimmings, City and Guilds certificate in rodent destruction, experienced fish eater, three years service on the clock, one careful owner, two scratched children, four damaged curtains, highly recommended, as new."

It seemed a good, competent, cat but it rejected us; not intelligent enough for it perhaps. We slunk away and made inquiries at an organisation that dealt with the safeguarding and disposal of cats to good homes.

"We haven't got the kind of cat you want but if we did manage to find one, we would have to look at you and see if you were both suitable as owners." said an official. "If so, you would have to sign a document stating that you would take all possible care of the animal and that you would agree to regular visits from one of our people to see that the cat was in good order."

"Very reasonable," I thought and said that I would be willing to sign anything—even unto half my kingdom—for the right kind of feline to pace the Morris territories with a purposeful tread and keep mice and burglars at bay.

As it happened we did not need to draw on the resources of that excellent organisation since my wife spotted an advertisement in a shop window stating in effect that an intelligent, active, well-spoken, good-mannered, middle-class female cat from the Marchmont area of Edinburgh was available to owners who knew quality when they saw it.

We called at the house and were shown another example of what could be termed a standard cat model. It seemed well-sprung, adequately upholstered, was a mouser of proven ability and had been the pet of a young women who, because of the terms of her let, was no longer allowed to keep a cat in her flat.

It took one look at us and tried to make a bolt for it but after a few seconds frantic chase, it was seized and held up for inspection. It did not exactly have the educational qualifications I wanted but the lady in temporary charge of it assured us that it was willing to learn, had been privately educated and could be given an excellent character reference. It was a very fastidious cat, had been used almost exclusively to female company but would no doubt get used to anyone of the male persuasion.

Surrendering to sudden impulse, we took it and before it could get its guard up, bundled it into the car, warned it not to cry because it wouldn't do any good and drove at full possible speed through the darkened Edinburgh streets to our house where we released it with a curt order to "settle down."

It didn't but gave a superb imitation of some panic-driven creature racing in front of a forest fire. Every few seconds there was a whirr and a blurr of movement as it dashed from room to room, now under beds, now scrambling over wardrobes, anon trying to hide behind or erect a barrier between us and it with plastic bags and cardboard boxes in cupboards and again leaping onto coffee tables and leaving behind overturned pot plants, scattered magazines and cries from us of "here kitty, kitty,"—a phrase that it treated with fathomless contempt.

Eventually, the movement slowed down and halted under a bed. After we had tried friendly persuasion, then a cautious brush pole to get it out, and failed at each attempt, we let the cat—which answered when it felt like it and that was seldom, to the name of Tania—sharply alone.

Later, it came out of hiding and warily inspected its new owners. It took to my wife with some alacrity but regarded me with deep, nervous, suspicion. Every time I talked to it, asking for instance if the present weather suited it, the cat would give a sudden leap in the air and shoot away like a fired projectile.

That hurt me somewhat because most animals get along with me and dogs often look on me as the best thing since the manufacture of rubber bones. That would have not been so bad but for the fact that the cat also seems to be something of a literary critic.

At one stage in the adjustment period, it crept into my study, jumped on the desk, took one look at an article I was writing, gave a screech that seemed to mingle disbelief with despair and fled to hide in some dark corner from which it could be persuaded to leave only after reassurances from me that I would not subject it to such an ordeal again and that there was a bowl of cream for it on the first turning on the right after leaving the cupboard.

The other day plumbers arrived to clear ice-blocked pipes

in our house, their bawling voices and hammer blows on metal only confirming to Tania that males were to be avoided at all costs.

She began racing from room to room again. "Here, that's an active cat you've got missus," said an honest artisan as she darted over his tool box and between his legs, leapt on to the kitchen sink, knocked over a cup and shot away into the domestic yonder leaving a series of thumps and crashes in her turbulent wake.

After that incident, tragedy occurred. I was engaged in fending off a white Persian that was trying to invade our house and left the front door open as I drove it down the garden path.

"The cat has gone," announced my wife with a stricken air. Tania, it seemed, sensing the fresh air of freedom, had made a bolt from the domestic H-block. "It's out there in all this cold," wailed my wife. "I knew this would happen. Fate doesn't want us to have a cat."

Stung by her reproach, twinged by conscience and driven by anxiety lest I saw a stiffly-frozen feline in the purlieus, I paced the streets shouting in vain for the escapee as one who calls the cattle home across the sands of Dee.

Disconsolately, we spent a morning in the city brooding on our loss and wondering what to tell the cat's previous owner. We returned to find it just emerging from a dark cupboard with a look of bland innocence in its eyes. It ignored me and rushed to greet my wife with a cry that indicated gladness and a request for food.

How do I feel? An underdog, but one with an urge to chase a cat up a tree and keep it there.

4

Bright as a button stick

THE other Sunday as I was driving along a road
skirting the Pentland Hills near Edinburgh, I saw a
bunch of young warriors, clad in complete Army
camouflage garb with matching rifles and automatic
weapons and with faces blackened to give them a
resemblance to some chorus in the old *Black and White
Minstrel Show.*

A fine body of men they seemed, giving an impression of
high energy and determination and who could have taken
their places in my old bunch, the Royal Army Mobile
Stationery Corps, with only a few questions asked.

I lowered the window as I passed and saluted them but if
they paid any attention I missed it. Ah well, I thought, as
they moved at the double in a rhythmic clatter of bootsteps,
one can hardly expect them to have time for an old Army
retread like myself who does not want gratitude but only
kept the sun from setting on the British Empire, the old flag
flying, the peace of the border line—wherever it might be—
and maintained stoutly and against heavy odds his place in
the queue for the cocktail bar of the New Stanley Hotel,
Nairobi, as well as going "over the top" for the prize of some
stale, lead-heavy NAAFI bun and tea that tasted like—and
may well have included—paint thinner.

As is well known I do not like to write or talk about my
Army experience even though I am a piece of Imperial
history writ small but occasionally I believe that a
revelation or two about my—generally peaceful—military

26

past will recall to older people, and make younger ones realise, the glory of the days when I personally stood alone on the square at the Gordon Barracks, Aberdeen, presenting—in a manner of speaking—arms and heard the words of the sergeant bellowing to recruits in a chill north-easter: "And that is not how to do it."

Sometimes when on my couch I lie in pensive mood I wonder whether, if the call came, I would be able to slot myself back into columns of threes, ground, port and pick up arms in a way that would strike terror into this country's foes.

As a grenade thrower I was adjudged more vigorous than skilful, as a marksman I took years off the lives of those warriors on the butts who led a precarious existence raising and lowering targets, pointing out bulls, near misses and wides, the latter being shown prominently on my score card and which gave the lads beside the targets first-hand and valuable experience of near battle conditions.

I did become expert in one military practice—changing step on the march. One did this at the command with a kind of tap-dance, and balletic motion and immediately I knew, as I executed the steps, that I had come into my own. My change of step sometimes produced a change of heart in NCOs when dealing with me, and once one came up to me—I'll swear there were tears in his heavy-duty, field-service eyes—and said: "If I had 10,000 men who could change step like you Private Morris, we could go through the Iron Curtain like a hot bayonet through butter."

Great words, great days, and I only mention them so that readers will know the calibre of the man who recalls them and appreciate him now so as to avoid any rush.

The other day, my ears pricked like that of an old

warhorse at a bugle call when I heard on the radio that a plan to recreate the Home Guard—Grandad's Army—is being considered by the Ministry of Defence. It is felt that a volunteer body of men could play an important role in a third world war by guarding vital civil and military installations thus freeing fully trained troops for demanding tasks. Its members would be trained to use firearms although they would not be allowed to keep their guns at home.

I remember, as if it were the day before yesterday, the long, hot summer of 1940 when the smell of wet sandbags was in every street, when blue birds were over the white cliffs of Dover, the washing had been temporarily kept from the Siegfried Line and the first of the formations of the Home Guard were being formed.

A few of my friends, older than me, were just able to get themselves into the somewhat untidy ranks and took their places alongside the middle-aged, the grey-bearded, the arthritic and the varicose-veined, thus procuring themselves a uniform in which they could swank before the girls and a rifle that they could slap, bang, shoulder and sometimes—greatly daring—even fire.

I used to watch them on parade getting military backbone instilled into them—"You may have broke your cubmistresses hearts but you won't break mine"—saluting in column of threes, diagonal marching to and fro, marking time, standing at ease and carrying out various other actions deemed useful for stopping the Nazi hordes on the beaches and landing grounds. But most of all I watched them change step on the march, to me the epitome of military punctilio.

I tried to get into the Home Guard on the compassionate grounds that not being able to change step was causing me great distress but was gently advised by a recruiting officer to try the Army Cadets which were looking for able-bodied youngsters, from infants to those whose chins were about to be enriched with one appearing hair, to form a last lollipop line of defence should the Hun attempt to set his foul jackboots on our land and attempt to breathe our air.

I offered my services, was accepted and was given for drill purposes a very small forage cap and a very large rifle—almost as long as I was tall—held together by wire.

When I and other children used to make our way with our rifles—last used, I now suspect, in the third Afghan war—people would shake their heads and comment that Britain was not just scraping the barrel but using the wood as well. Once I remember dragging my rifle along behind me—it needed all my strength to lift it on to my shoulders and keep it there for about ten seconds before my knees buckled—and hearing an adult say to another. "Now I see what they mean by total war."

We had a drill instructor, a Boer War veteran who always claimed he had blown the "charge" at Magersfontein—although I was told later that he had never been nearer the front than corporal's mess in Cape Town—who used to encourage the mixed infants on with word and gesture. "Bright as button-sticks you kids are," he would say. "Chin in, chest out, show President Kruger a healthy brisket. Remember, four rounds for the enemy and one round for yourself if there's any chance of the Boer women getting at you. Stand straight now and no crying in the ranks."

Across in Europe, the massed ranks of the Nazis were concentrating in Northern France. Aloft, incumbent on the summer air, was the RAF making Southern England ankle-deep in bits of Luftwaffe; around our coasts the Royal Navy was in position, and up in Edinburgh the Army Cadets were flexing their tiny muscles and pink fingers, about-turning, slow and quick marching, painfully attempting to ease springs on the bolts of antediluvian rifles, but never, oh never, changing step on the march.

I spoke to our instructor about this grave lack in our tactical training. "What's this? What's this?" harrumphed the ancient warrior. "Stand up straight, arms by your sides, chin in, chest out, when you're speaking to me, laddie, and call me 'sergeant'."

He listened carefully to my complaint and said he was a non-believer in changing step on the march. Unsound movement, even dangerous, he had seen brave lads going into action, changing step, and even saluting on the march under heavy fire, and it had done them no good at all. "Back to the ranks, laddie," he said. "Bright as a button stick you are." Fortunately for me, the Army did not share his doubts about that movement and I changed steps time, with and without number.

Have no doubt that if need be I will either offer my services in a new Home Guard or organise a small columnar one myself, armed with nuclear-power cross-bows firing arrows tipped with fulminate of mercury. Rest assured we shall be changing step in the most menacing way. Watch the Ruskies or any other such nation turn in their tracks and flee.

5

Day of the promising tradesman

DO you know how I regard our tradesmen these days? As very promising people. They may vary in efficiency, in dedicated application to work and in appearance—ranging from the clean and neatly-dressed to those who look as if they have just emerged from cleaning a ship's bilges—but what they all appear to have in common is an uncanny ability to promise to do a job on a certain day, begin it at an agreed time and complete it on schedule and then, with impressive and unfailing regularity, fail to turn up.

I have been attempting to persuade a young joiner to do business with me in connection with a small but necessary job in the house. When he turned up, appraised the work, sat in a corner, licked a blunt pencil and on the back of a fag packet did various sums in estimation of materials to be supplied and hours to be worked, he seemed almost to be pawing the ground in eagerness to earn an honest coin of the realm. "No sweat squire," he said in the engaging parlance of the working man. "Soon get this done. Look a treat when finished. Guarantee a good job, see you next Monday morning at 9 o'clock, Bob's your uncle. Ta Ta for now. I'll see myself out."

I liked his brisk, business-like approach and firm, manly handshake and the way he looked straight into my eyes without a tremor. He may have diffused an odour of wood shavings, fag-ends and old putty but there, I declared roundly to myself, was a man who would turn out a highly

31

polished piece of fine grain square deal.

Monday at 9 a.m. was soon replaced by 9.30 a.m. and was followed in the fullness of time by 11. At 11.30 I phoned his number and was answered by a lady who appeared to be trying to calm a squalling infant and a barking dog. "Boab?" she answered in the vernacular. "He's no' in," and to make matters clear even to the meanest intelligence, she added: "He's oot. Oan a joab . . . in Fife."

That depressing information seemed to produce a terrible effect on the child who burst into a yell that sounded like a miniature gas explosion. I shared its sadness over daddy's absence. What, I asked the lady, had happened to the schedule that had placed the esteemed Mr Morris and his small but profitable joab first on the day's work. The lady disclaimed knowledge of or responsibility for her husband's absence from my house.

He moved, she indicated, in strange ways his joinery to perform. I ought, she added, to phone him at night when apparently he could be found slumped over the telly, the sweat of honest toil on his brow.

I did so. "Remember me?" I asked. "Mr Morris. Work to begin promptly at 9 a.m. No sweat. Bob's your uncle." There was a long pause while the man's memory mists were stirred. "Got you," he said with the triumphant air of a cross-examining counsel. "Small chap, big glasses and sort of balding." "You could put it that way," I said stiffly, "but not if you expect future valuable and esteemed work from me."

There was a sound that appeared to be a hand clutching a sweat-stained brow. "Gosh, I meant to phone you about that. Had this important contract come up. Matter of urgency, couldn't get out of it, hotel owner wouldn't take

No for an answer. Look, will tomorrow do? Good. See you then, 9 o'clock. On the dot. All the best squire. Apologies and all that. Knew you'd understand."

The next day failed to draw that Pimpernel-elusive man to my house. His wife revealed gloomily that he was joining pieces of wood in Peebles, for what purpose who could say? "Tell him the squire phoned and that I'd like to hear from him sometime," I said cryptically and hung up as mysteriously as I had rung.

Of course, Boab—whether he is my uncle or otherwise— is only one of many gentlemen of craft who nowadays appear unable or unwilling to carry out work as promised. Those who have had building work carried out in their houses and who have spent frantic hours trying to get some plumber, plasterer or joiner to complete tasks that they had been promised would be finished by a certain time will have experienced the exquisite tortures of expectations continually blasted by the wind of changed tradesmen's minds.

A friend who has recently had an extension to his house completed after months of delay, told me brokenly that at one point, when his house resembled the ruins of a First World War French battlefield village, the joiner said he could not carry on with the work until the plumber had completed his stint.

When contacted, the plumber claimed in an affronted way that the contractor had neglected to inform him about the time schedule but promised to contact the boss to confirm the joiner's claim. When days passed and my friend phoned the contractor, he was met with a hot and testy denial. "I've told him repeatedly that he had to get the work finished as soon as possible," the anguished man yelled.

"You tell him to get cracking or he's had it." For a time my friend became a sort of middleman soother and interpreter of the two men's assertions and denials and after about a week, with the threat in the pipeline of an immediate removal of the plumber from the workforce, that work was completed while the contractor went off as a character witness for the plasterer who was in dock on a drunk while driving trial.

When that valuable man was cleared of the charge of being plastered the work was again held up because the electrician who had vowed almost tearfully that he would complete rewiring on time, blew a promissory fuse and left the work undone until an apparently more rewarding contract had been fulfilled.

Such unfulfilling tradesmen are bad enough but what rubs pepper into the contractual wounds is the attitude some of these men adopt when customers remonstrate, even mildly, against their dilatory techniques.

The representative of a firm which had promised and failed to supply men to lay carpets I had bought from them some time ago, took grave exception to me pointing out that I had waited at home for two days for the carpets to arrive and would he mind giving me a firm date this time and sticking to it. The man's attitude was that of a haughty seigneur resenting criticism from an underling. "If you think we're at the beck and call of every customer to arrive just when they want, you've another guess coming . . . sir." But for the fact that I had foolishly paid for the carpets I would have informed him that my other guess was that he had lost a customer. As it was I hoped he would give me another chance to adjust my ungrateful attitudes and to develop much-needed patience.

Boab, I may say, has now completed the job after being nailed by me in a final act of desperate pleading. Of course I promised to pay him on the dot, "toot," as he would say "sweet," Bob is his uncle and that means . . . eventually.

6

Figures in a mental landscape

AS the days shorten and the autumnal equinoctial winds of little or no change shrill along the valleys of the mind and toss and tumble yellowing leaves that could never be turned over even when new, it is time once more for the wanderers and watchers of the emotional landscape to seek out the many wonders and secrets of the mind that can be glimpsed only by those who know where to look in the tangled unanalytical cerebral foliage and in the labyrinthine byways of the subconscious.

This, of course, is one of the most rewarding periods of the year for the mental countryside lover, writes Scrimshank. Snide is out in the usual shades of snigger brown, envy is still green while rooted dislike covers a large area and is often difficult to remove along with the hair bristles of deep chagrin.

Herb o' ill-grace has made its first coy appearance and acrimony is all the rage in the lower foothills of the distant piques. Quite a sight you will agree for the keen-eyed observer and of course there is more to come.

If we take this old mental rut, marked out by sticks in the mud and noting as we walk along, the tread of old remarks and the delved brow-type parallels, perhaps made by some winged chariot of mental time, we can see an early forming clump of stab-in-the-back alongside a small group of faded friendship and forget-me-quick as well as a cluster of I'm-all-right jacked up against a small hedge against inflated writing, the latter cluster surprisingly late for the time of the year but still blooming true.

Quiet. Don't move a mental muscle. Don't even blink a mind's eye. In the distance you can see a small buck passing a doubting nag carking for care in a clump of late-flowering worry. No, no. To the right, past the clump of tangled logic near that bank of hidden doubts. Yes, voices down please. I haven't seen one of these passing for some time. Usually the buck stops here to take the can or moral responsibility laid out for it. Times are changing though; perhaps you've noticed it, and a fast buck like that seldom or never comes my way nowadays.

Isn't nature wonderful especially a nature like mine? Ah, here—don't step on it please—is a patch of prose, purpling nicely. This, as you must know, seldom sees the light of day but it is a persistent growth and one cannot help admiring its naive tenacity and dawn-innocent profusion.

As we carry on our ego trip, noting in the languid hang-dog air how distant sounds travel and make, for instance, a far-off train of thought appear to be running out of steam just beside us, we hear the melancholy notes of a crying need snivelling for an ale-pale night jar.

We are in luck, as I thought we would be. Overhead—keep well under cover now—we can see flight of soaring thoughts leaving the mind perhaps never to return until the spring and possibly not even then. You will note please the typical derisive V-shaped formation as they pass beyond the inspiration skyline. Lovely, eh? Makes you wish some psychiatric bard was on hand to capture the scene in his native analytical jargon wild.

Look, this is of much interest; keep moving to the right please as I speak. It is an early example of monumental folly built as we can see of dropped bricks, heart's bloodstone and topped by a small bell or clanger. There is no indication of when the monument was erected but from part of the faint 500 lines written in neck brass on one side and half obscured by mental moss and which seem to read: "I must not throw chalk at Miss Hilda Rampart, primary 4C," the monument would seem to commemorate a behavioural aberration of incredible antiquity.

If we go round this bend or twist, we arrive at some outstanding views of the spacious contours of the inspirational fields through which a small spring runs a rusty brown, bearing with it half-formed ideas, discarded plots for three-volume novels and the detritus of a thousand rejected sentences. In the distance you will see vast tracts of cerebral marshlands across which at night you might spot the fitful wandering shape of an occasional original idea, that gets lost in the mental mist.

Perhaps, too, you will hear the mournful cry and heavy splash of a doggerel descending on clumsy metrical feet.

How, peaceful it is. Across the area of Rope's End wood, the only sound one hears is the soothing rasp of a wise saw and modern instance making shoulder chips to store up future columns. In the distance, the pale psychological sun illuminates and makes strangely noble the rusting skeletal structure of derelict heroic couplets and incomplete iambic pentameters which stand alongside ancient experimental columns, looking like some abandoned idea by Isambard Kingdom Brunel, the riveting prose rusted and gossamer ideas now as faded and wasted as battle banners hung in some sombre cathedral.

Never mind. There is an inspiriting tang in the air. It comes as it always does from the acrid smoke of burning issues, indignant readers' letters, contention bones and other controversial and instantly combustible material.

As the opinion shades fall, we leave the mental landscape with its curious but vigorous ecology, the inspiration gained from the warp and woof of the pageant of its life no doubt sustaining us for the rest of the year and leaving us with the thought that while you can lead a gift horse to a stream it is a long worm that has no turning.

We may not know what that means—if anything—but brooding over it may help us to pass many a weary night until we can come to the mental landscape in spring with its exuberant Freudian growths, Adlerian outcrops and Jungian byways and a host of other things too good to miss. I look forward to taking you all round it. Book now and avoid the rush.

7

Marx and his brothers

THE revelation that Karl Marx, author of "Das Kapital," the less well-known "Zur Kritik der Politischen Oekonomie" and other gripping, action-packed works that have drawn children from their play and old men from their chimney corner spitoons, failed to become a British citizen comes as no surprise to me—a fact which of course will come as no surprise to readers.

It may not be generally known, and indeed it all now seems like a dream to me, but as a somewhat politically precocious child, I was actually dandled on the great man's vast intellectual knee while he crooned, in a voice suggestive of a Polish ox-cart squeaking over a rutted road, sad songs of agrarian disturbance near Tobolsk, and whispered somewhat, unintelligible English translations of his "Misere de la Philosophie" into my child's shell-pink ear.

Far from confining his literary activities to the reading room of the British Museum, Marx made many journeys to the land of the mountain and the flood, visiting Edinburgh from time to time where he stayed at the house of an elderly uncle of mine, a little-known but highly-intense political thinker given to periodic outbursts of fury—coinciding with the appearance of certain sunspots—against the monarchy, Gladstone, Irish Home Rule, etc. which amounted to very little when you came to sift matters.

Marx, or "Charlie" as he came to be known in the crude vernacular of the time, was, if I may coin a phrase, a gentle giant, or at least he seemed so to me, wearing sober clothes of a curious Continental cut which smelled faintly of ink, snuff and stale dialectics. He spoke English with a heavy Teutonic accent rather similar to that used for prestige purposes by Henry Kissinger.

Not only Marx but many other intellectuals of weight, not only of mind and body but utterance, came to the house to discuss matters that were simply on everyone's lips those days—the class struggle, the theory of capitalist appropriation and accumulation of surplus value, the material evolution of society and, of course, Marx's eternal, and to tell the truth, somewhat tiresome requests to get people to sponsor his naturalisation papers.

I can remember even through the memory mists my uncle introducing some new guest to the assembled company whose beards made them look like wild creatures peering through the under-growth: "I want you to meet the boys," he would say, "Heine, Marx, Proudhon, Engels, Plekhanov and Bakunin who is in the anarchist business."

These were great nights, the old house ringing with laughter as quips about historical materialism, material determinism and determined material historicism rent the air and the sound of robust old revolutionary ditties made the rafters ring.

Of all that august company, I think I liked old Fred Engels best. It was because of his unswerving patience that at an early age I learned to lisp the opening paragraphs of the Communist Manifesto of 1848 which my aunt tried to set to music with, alas, little success.

Plekhanov and Bukunin I never cared for. "Ruskies," as one of the servants described them, "and nasty with it." There was, I noted, invariably snow on their boots even on the mildest nights. I once received, I regret to say, a distinct boot on a portion of my rearward anatomy that I would rather not mention as I played around the feet of the assembled guests while they were working out plans to speed the decay of the bourgeoisie. I immediately suspected Bakunin but Plekhanov's face, twisted in an evil Slavonic grin, confirmed my worst fears about his maleficent nature.

Sometimes in the purple city dusk I would creep up on Mr Marx as he drank his Russian tea with a cube of sugar in his mouth, making a noise like a muted hurricane between his well-shaped revolutionary teeth.

He seemed sad. Yet another application for naturalisation had been rejected by the bigots of Scotland Yard. But despite his dejection he would always find time to tell me some fairy story involving perhaps a magic value-creating power gained by a humble peasant which he would use with devastating effect against oppressive landlords, proprietors of London East End sweat shops and which would ensure the revolutionary determination and eternal victory of the workers against the forces of capitalism and reaction.

Eventually my aunt would remind him gently that it was time to go to his revolutionary hot bed lovingly prepared by her and which included inflammatory sheets and a pillow stuffed with tracts from the first, second and third internationals. Off he would go, gentle as a lamb, excluding a faint spray of cigar ash and Continental-type dandruff as he did so.

My uncle, a man of sudden inspirations, once told Marx that while he was only talking off the top of his head, he thought there was an inevitability about Socialism and eventually of full Communism. The latter had to be understood as a classless, collective order in which the

010 871 1440612

THE GEEST LINE

Bar Voucher. Date......................19

	AMOUNT £

Signature... **£**

PASSENGERS ARE REQUESTED TO SIGN FOR ALL ITEMS
PURCHASED FROM THE BAR DAILY.

Stuart Macgregor.

43

social product was distributed according to needs and in which the state, law, money and the concept of economic value had lost their functions and had therefore "withered away." I remember Marx thinking deeply about that for some time and saying he thought there might be an idea for a book in it.

He eventually lived in London permanently where, I believe, he made his name in writing. I remember one day he put an arm around me affectionately and said: "Ve vill make von big Socialist out of you yet mein liebchen." He was wrong in that as he was in many of his other prophecies. Politically I am now slightly to the right of Genghis Khan but despite that old Charlie Marx will always find a place in my heart.

8

Blank looks for Miss Brodie

IT was the time of tinkling teacups in Edinburgh when behind the lace-curtained enclaves of middle-class respectability in Morningside, Newington and other refined settlements in the city, those residents with some leisure to refresh their elegant tissues were soothing themselves with tea and comforting themselves with cream-laced carbohydrates and respectable Scottish biscuits of an austere, strengthening and wholesome nature.

In one of the city's art galleries the creme de la creme of Edinburgh schoolchildren—pupils of the Marcia Blaine School for Girls, an august independent educational establishment of a nature beyond limited comprehensive comprehension—were being efficiently put through the continuing process of having old heads placed on their young shoulders by no less a skilled technician at the task than Miss Jean Brodie, a teacher who, when seen in a certain light, looked like an angel fondly regarding the madonna and child in an Italian Renaissance painting and at other times resembled Charlotte Corday about to pierce the ego of Marat in his revolutionary bath.

Miss Brodie's pupils were of course vastly informed on many subjects irrelevant and sometimes diametrically opposed to the authorised curriculum—motor-cycle maintenance, Zen Buddhism, the art of cannabis plant arranging, the practice of thuggee, the light and heavy thoughts of North Korean president Kim Il Sung and how to tie a clove hitch around the jugular of any presumptuous

45

young male who attempted—as sometimes happened even in respectable and deferential Edinburgh—to force his heavy-breathing, pimple-faced attentions on them or—as sometimes happened—vice-versa.

The girls, neat in their conformist frayed denims, wearing badges of innocent eroticism on their jackets and shirts, their expertly made-up young faces shining with gratification at being let off boring arithmetic, stupefying English and smelly old science, the latter under the draconian death's head direction of Miss Gaunt, were doing their girlish best to feign interest at the Scottish Art Council's Gallery in Charlotte Square to see the latest exhibition of "minimalist art" to reach Edinburgh.

It was Miss Brodie's object to take a young girl's mind and by a process of educational brain surgery, open it and stuff in a tag-rag, tail-bob of information, then stitch the loose folds of the mind back into place, an achievement which she described as "opening up new horizons."

What confronted the children now, not even Miss Brodie's lectures on the ill-breeding of showing even genteel surprise could have prepared them to accept without an interrogative or baffled gasp from their cunningly-rosebudded lips. The exhibition consisted entirely of blank canvasses with coloured borders. Everyone except Miss Brodie tittered.

Monica Douglas, a prefect, who was secretly collecting the Encyclopaedia of Sex in 250 weekly instalments and who would take to drink in chapter three, frowned at the eruption of irreverence towards art, a subject which was Miss Brodie's confessed passion apart from that for her lover who had fallen in Flanders, knocked down, it was rumoured in the cloakroom, by a taxi during a package holiday. She sternly hushed the girls into a respectful silence.

Miss Brodie's views on art were firm but flexible. At one time she did not believe there had been a single significant artistic development since the death of Giotto but she had swiftly moved with the trend-setting times and if any art appeared to be above the heads of the masses, she could be relied on to reach the required altitude.

"Mayree Macgregor," she asked a girl, shaped like a badly-made Cornish pastie and with a face the colour of a Van Gogh sunset, "come out here and tell us what you see in these superb examples of Gestalt perceptual psychology as applied to abstract art."

The blankness of the paintings were mirrored in Mary's small raisin-like eyes—she was to become a ravishing beauty in page 469 and marry a Texan toothbrush millionaire—out of which tears of embarassement fell like sleet. She groped for her handkerchief unfortunately up the leg of her knickers and was led off to spend the rest of the time sobbing convulsively and looking furtively over her handkerchief to see if there were any nude statues with fig leaves on them as a change from blank paintings on blank walls.

Miss Brodie then talked about Jo Baer, the artist whose surface articulations, she claimed, proceeded by the discovery of theorems or precepts correlative to intuitions or sub-realities, and, of course, so on.

Many people—"Sandee stop picking your teeth with the catalogue and try and sit up straight; you'll need a corset before you're 16"—were ignorant about modern art like Councillor Cornelius Waugh, leader of the Conservative Group of Edinburgh District Council, who had criticised the paintings and could no doubt see nothing in them. But people like that were not the creme de la creme and only stirred up trouble in their rate-payer-subsidised municipal teacups.

Some people had even said that the paintings were not art—"Jenny, do you have fleas? Well stop scratching yourself and look up the definition of art when you get home," but art was only in the eye of the beholder. Art was beyond man, beyond time, perhaps beyond even the universe itself. Art was everywhere, art was nowhere if you could not see it. She hoped that what she said was clear because she would be asking questions later about it.

Afterwards the girls went to the Richard Demarco Gallery in the High Street where the works of Roger Kite showed a soaring of the artistic spirit resulting in more apparently blank canvases.

Miss Brodie gathered her flock around her and asked one girl with a face like a young walnut what she thought of the paintings. "They're not about anything, Miss Broaaadie," she faltered, "just sort of blank."

"Blankness is all nowadays," said her teacher. "In blankness you must see primeval chaos, the structure of civilisation, the final implosion of the universe, inner and outer space or even Shirley Temple singing "Animal Crackers in my Soup." In fact I can see anything I like and like anything I see. That is what art is."

The girls sighed, wishing they were with Miss Gaunt and separating iron filings. Miss Brodie left them to go home on a bus where not one man put his hand on her Botticelli-type knee—the girls believed you could get fleas that way—and no invite came to pose for her art teacher male friend. She was in her prime and if the glass of gin in her hand meant anything she was going to get even more primed now. There was an art in that; there was of course an art in everything.

9

Trying the year for size

PEOPLE have often told me how well I carry my years—not of course that I carry too many compared with the big-time weight-lifters like Methuselah (969 years if a Biblical day). Cainan (910 years at the final quivering lift and lowering) and Noah who was doubtless a lithe-limbed 600 years old when low cloud, excessive precipitation and emergency flooding conditions covered the earth, and 950 years when he went into permanent dry dock.

I am, however, mature enough to carry as well my weight of life's cliches and am therefore aware that I am old enough to know better, my mind, that there is no fool like an middle-aged fool, that things, are fairly certain to get better provided they do not take a turn for the worse, that if one door closes another could slam, that it is often darkest before the false dawn but that it isn't a bad old world if you can keep your feet on the ground, your head above water but not in the clouds, your eye on the ball, back to the wall and your nose clean on the grindstone.

I also know by instinct as well as experience that this is the time when I get myself fitted for my new year and try it on for shape, size and texture.

I always get my years wholesale from the old Anno Domini factory run by F. Time & Co., and I can personally recommend that skilled old tailor and cutter for an uncanny ability to hack out from the most unpromising 12 months an excellent, form-fitting year to suit the most discerning

49

people who want good, hard-wearing yet trend-flecked, minutely-stitched material.

As always the place was crowded with customers getting the first of the months draped around them and I can tell you the time fluff was flying about the fitting rooms as people discarded thankfully the crumpled, threadbare, shapeless old year and scrutinised themselves critically in the new.

They know me at F. Time as a hard-to-please gent who appreciates a good-quality year when he wears it and who will not be fobbed off with some of the shoddy muck that passes for weeks and months these days and are over before you realise that you have had them.

Old Time's aeon-crinkled features crumpled into wide smile when he saw me fingering some old-fashioned material "Ah Mr Morris, trust you to get to a quality year. That stuff," he said, opening the Charleston-flecked, Al Jolson-voiced year, "is your genuine 1927. A minute was made to last then, like this lot," he said, indicating some left-over 1938. "If you had an hour in these years you knew about it, especially if it belonged to a Scottish Sunday. Look how all the months are stitched cunningly together with heavy-duty weeks, don't get these sort of years now and you can't get the young month pressers and minute cutters to work the same hours. Heavy, riddled with quality, sir, these are time weights for no man nowadays."

Reluctantly I took my gaze from the styles of long ago and while I don't often criticise the old boy's workmanship, this time I let him have it straight above the long, white beard about the previous year. "I had to get it extensively re-altered after the first few weeks, didn't like what was cut out for me, didn't fancy the gros gain in behavioural pattern and the silver lining fell out before I realised I'd been given one."

Mr Time clicked his tongue with ancient sympathy and commented: "You're lucky. Some people's years eventually look like old Portland Blue Cement bags; it's the way they use them, of course." I leaned forward to hear the better as he bent over the crumpled remains of my old year.

"Ah yes. Here it frayed at the themes and there I would say you lost the thread of your remarks off the cuff. Still, it hung together extremely well and frankly it still looks in good shape for another 12 months without drastic re-alteration."

I shook my head firmly disturbing a few time flies waiting for who knew what on my shoulders. "I want a completely new year, repetitions of old ones are bad for me even although I admit you do get used to the days and the weeks fit like old, worn slippers."

The ancient craftsman took out his tape measure and flicked it across me like a chameleon's tongue. "Chap like you needs a well-cut year that will give him a distinguished look even in a crowded hour that us worth an age without a name.

"Youngsters can get away with slipshod time tailoring but you have to be careful not to show the minutes rumpling and the fortnights riding up as you get beyond the first three months."

He displayed the shelves for something to suit my chromatic taste. "Something fairly cheerful this year to make people think I'm working an income-tax dodge," I said pointing out a colour that I liked. "Ah, a bolt from the blue," said Mr Time taking down the fancy material. "Lots of people with strong nerves like this; it keeps them on their toes which us good for the overhang of the months above the instep and there is enough stuff to make some nice turn-ups for the books."

I shook my head and chose a quiet but watchful grey in traveller's check to enable me to blend into the background of Edinburgh and other settlements of refinement and civilisation on a normal commercial day. "How do you like your hours," asked the greybeard his mouth full of spare seconds which he pinned neatly into place.

"The trend now is short in the working week and with a long, flared matching leisure extension," he added. "I'll have them," I said, relying on the old boy to see me right for posterity and beyond.

"Minutes?" he asked. "Oh, give me the usual 60 seconds-worth," I said, "no need to throw tradition overboard entirely." "Months?" he queried, making curious chalk hieroglyphics on some material he was shaping for my future outlook. "I want them to pass quickly when I'm bored and slowly when I'm enjoying myself. Fit in some time off for traditional industrial disputes, waiting at bus queues and airports and well . . . just whatever you think best yourself."

Carefully 1978 was fitted on. It seemed too big; the pocket for my pride was in place, there was plenty of material to let out for ego extension if necessary but it seemed to lack shape. "Don't worry, Mr Morris," said Mr Time, his gnarled hand screwing up the months behind my back, "it fits you beautifully in front and you'll find it will grow tighter as the days wear on."

I stepped out into icy, snow-filled Edinburgh; 1978 flapped cheerfully around me and I expect I would get used to it somehow and might even—who knows?—get to like it.

10

Hole truth

AS one who regards watching the British road worker going about his tasks with pick, shovel, drill and copy of some sporting paper as a constant source of entertainment, I was happy to read in a newspaper report that a man has been appointed to investigate the matter in depth at the instigation of the Government.

Professor Michael Horne, formerly Beyer Professor of Civil Engineering at Manchester University and who has been one of Britain's experts on bridge construction, has been appointed by Mrs Lynda Chalker, Minister of Transport, to head an independent review into the 1,800,000 holes dug every year by electricity, gas, water and telephones to repair their lines or pipes.

Now that television companies are about to lay hundreds of miles of TV cables, the Government are keen that the quality of work is improved when the holes are filled in.

The report said that during an investigation into the problem last year it was shown that poor workmanship led to a deterioration in road conditions for all road users, particularly those on bicycles and motor bikes, delays to traffic while the excavations were being carried out and an increase in the frequency with which roads required maintenance treatment.

According to the report the professor need travel no further than the Greater Manchester area which with 100,000 new holes a year can boast—if that is the word—one of the most scarred road networks in Britain.

Although this column prides itself on its instant and accurate information, provided with no expense spared, it was not able yesterday to get facts and figures about Edinburgh's excavations either in whole or in part but I suspect that we are not much behind—if at all—the total of that illustrious Lancashire city.

There are times when Edinburgh resembles a large termite mound riddled with holes which, many citizens believe, are often placed strategically to ensure the maximum amount of traffic hold-up and pedestrian annoyance.

It is, however, especially during the summer months, when the city is filled with tourists looking at the capital's towers and turrets and buttresses and battlements, that the roads take on a gorgonzola appearance.

One day a street will be a normal thoroughfare bearing its load of vehicles and citizens hurrying on their business and pleasures. The next day a large and interesting crater will have appeared on it at the bottom of which workers will be seen, as actors on an apron stage, performing their various roles and not unaware of the audience in the gods staring down at them with concentrated scrutiny.

After a successful run of perhaps several weeks, the hole will close and the area will remain bleakly free of all entertainment for about a fortnight. Then, another travelling road show will be due to appear in the same place; word will be passed round the city crowds, ever ready for a free view of some municipal happening or a piece of street theatre organised by one of the main public utilities, and once more the curtain will go up on a scene of high drama or, as in many cases, low comedy.

I have been a member of the audience at many of these productions and I can tell those who have not, that you are taken right under the cosmetic surface of this city with its lofty artistic pretentions and its air of high morality and self-righteousness that smells of curiously-strong mints, acid drops, soor plooms and humbugs.

These shows certainly dig up the dirt and many a sensitive citizen has blushed at the earthy plots as well as the coarse structure of the demotic dialogue in the script.

There is nothing that your average Edinburgh audience likes better that a good settledown at the ramparts of the hole to watch the story unfold itself. There are some actors who seem to be on the theatrical circuit and who are instantly recognised and cheered or booed by the fickle crowd.

These are men, often heroically tattooed, with muscles like ship's hawsers who know the drill about a successful stage appearance. They will swagger on, flex their muscles for the benefit of the admiring girls with hairstyles like bloodstained carrots or partially-destroyed privet hedges, and add to the dramatic tension by pneumatically upturning large chunks of the real Edinburgh.

What a revelation it is. As well as being east windy and west endy, the city seems to be a mixture of various kinds of mud, obscene-looking pebbles and an unpleasant-jumbled network of pipes all no doubt bearing contents that gurgle and hiss in a manner I can hardly mention in what is after all a family column.

The cast revel in turning up a side of the city that would best be kept hidden. Here a worker will produce an ancient bottle with the vestigial remains of a label on it and the words "Campbell, Hope and King"—believed to be once a well-known city tonic—still on it. Items of unguessable, perhaps even unspeakable, use will be revealed in the hard, Scottish sunlight with a flourish by some undercover artist and the crowd will often give a ripple of applause and hope for fresh developments.

There are other workers who seem to have a passive role and who sit or lie in the crater, thoughtfully eating robust sandwiches while staring at the section in a newspaper that deals with the day's racing.

There is a kind of Dostoevskian or Chekhovian fatalism about these people, a hint of holey Russia where peasants sank to even greater depths of inertness and waited the knout, the revolution or even just the mood to stir them into action.

People often ask me what is my favourite time in Edinburgh. It is undoubtedly during the Festival when not only is the city above ground quivering with artistic action but the subterranean theatre is also in full blast. You might miss the opera, be unable to afford the ballet and not get a ticket for some pulsating Fringe show, but you can always rely on the city roads being open for practically incessant entertainment.

Of course, it is just a personal whim but I like a good underground show in any part of the High Street with motorists foaming and snarling around it to add an extra dramatic flavour to the scene, with perhaps a hint of gas escaping from some pipe being repaired, the scent of genuine Edinburgh mud so suggestive of ancient plum pudding and the cast going on about their tasks of bantering among themselves, exchanging smiles with or whistling at passing girls or artistically attempting to pick the winner of the 3.30 at Uttoxeter.

Some shrewd hole aficionados tell me, however, that any Princes Street production is always worth watching—some would never watch anything else—but I have revealed my choice and as a veteran and sensitive viewer, my opinion stands firmly on undermined soil.

I have no doubt that the entertainment value of Edinburgh's holes has been brought to the attention of Mr Frank Dunlop, director of Edinburgh Festival, with a view to what is essentially people's theatre being included in the official programme. I am also certain that Professor Horne will be up to see for himself what Edinburgh can dig up.

I implore all concerned, including the gas and electricity authorities and British Telecom to co-operate fully in this matter. Let's get the show on the road.

11

Ships that pass

READERS have often written to me saying how much they envy the kind of columnar life I lead, so divorced from that of the sweating, toiling and suffering masses. "I see you in your daily routine meeting princes, potentates, those who wear the purple of commerce, trade union nabobs and satraps as well, of course, as the common people such as journalists like yourself," one woman's letter stated.

Another wrote; "Not only do I think you know just about everything I believe you know just about everyone, that is everyone of note in the world."

Well, modesty and much else makes me disclaim those obviously well-meant statements but I can reveal that along these corridors of columnar power that I tread daily, people have passed whose names are, were, or certainly should have been, on everybody's lips.

Normally, I would name no names because discretion was at one time not only this column's telegraphic address but also in a loose manner of speaking my middle name. Now that I am on the subject, however, it might gratify many readers to know that while I have talked with crowds and kept what I am pleased to call my virtue, I have also walked with kings and kept the common touch.

It was with feelings of some sadness that I read the other day that Anna Anderson Manahan, who spent much of her life trying to establish the claim that she was the Grand Duchess Anastasia, daughter of the last Russian Tsar, died in the United States, aged 82.

I have in my possession a picture of Tsar Nicholas II's children, his four daughters and his son, the Tsarevitch Alexis. In the picture, Anastasia and the others, dressed in their court finery, face the camera with expressions on their young faces of mingled pride, shyness and innocence, all unsuspecting of the fate that awaited them in that house in Ekaterinburg.

It is the face of Anastasia that haunts me strangely. Had I seen it before, albeit when it had become lined with age and perhaps marked strangely by the downfall of her house and the old order in holy Russia?

Listen, for what I have to say is of much interest. I believe that for a time, all too short I now realise, a woman strangely resembling the grand duchess worked on this column doing a variety of menial tasks such as dusting the columnar desk with its detritus of stray adjectives and blunted adverbial clauses, making the occasional pot of tea for the staff—we always noted that she made it in the Russian fashion with a small, ornately decorated, coal-fired samovar—pouring the liquid without milk into a glass in which was also inserted a slice of lemon.

Many of us—myself included—used to comment jocularly but with kind intent on her exotic brew, so different from the coarse, khaki-coloured stuff, sharp as a bayonet thrust, made by willing but often unskilful minions.

The lady—she answered, though she was seldom asked, to the name of Mrs A. Purdie—would give a deep sigh and emit a labial-fricative sound of "oikh" which I have been told is an old Russian expression of deep resignation.

What also struck me about her was the grave and stately way she would curtsey to me when I entered my office to begin the columnar day, an action that smacked strongly of long years of court training in some austere school for scions of the autocracy.

Although she spoke with an accent many identified as being that of the Edinburgh Central parliamentary constituency, I always felt that I had in my midst someone who, for her own purposes, had adopted the technique of prospective mimicry and whose real accent was high-bred St Petersburg and which might even have been used to freeze the presumptuous Rasputin back into his vodka bottle.

Once, when I thought she looked particularly sad I offered her a glass of rare old tokay, once the property of the officer's mess of the Vossnessenk Lancers or it could have been from the Colonel's bin of the Elisabethgrad Hussars. A first sip seemed to bring a wintry gleam of recognition to her face, a memory of the old days, perhaps cruising on the imperial yacht or posing with the officers of the Tarnovsky regiment and sampling, though she was only a child, the regiment's famed claret.

I once hinted that I knew she was of the *ancient* regime but the lady, stopping in the middle of sweeping up the remains of sentence predicate that had been dropped on the floor and had broken, said in a phrase commonly used by Scottish ladies at that time: "Ye're daft." I was not, however, taken in.

Although I have been told that a Pablo Picasso once held a menial artistic role in the column and was partially responsible for creating the alleged representation of me at the top of this space, I never met the man although certain artistic graffiti in the prose purplers' wash-room suggest the all-too-facile touch of that Spanish mountebank.

There is very little doubt, in my mind at least, that Martin Bormann, one of Hitler's henchmen, worked on this column for a short time. While the *Daily Express* ran a series of stories which fooled no-one, except possibly the editor, that Bormann had been run to ground in South America while posing as Latin-looking businessman, I was absolutely certain that the fellow was here, working as a charge-hand on the production line that put buckram linings on nominative cases.

In all fairness, the man was affable enough; only his tendency to goose-step while showering in workers wash and recreation rooms and his occasional whistling of what sounded like the *Horst Wessel* song between his teeth, arousing any suspicion that he was not the full Scottish-born shilling.

He departed, giving me a gesture that was a combination of the Winston Churchill salute and the Nazi raised arm, and leaving behind, somewhat bafflingly, a copy of *Jane Eyre* in Sanscrit.

What others? Maxim Gorki, E. Hemmingway, W.B. Yeats and M. Proust have been here, I suspect, in spirit if not in body as have Bakunin, Proudhon and Enid Blyton.

One of the most mysterious workers in the columnar complex, however, was a small bearded man with the manners of a marquess or perhaps those of higher rank who said little to anybody and that in halting English with just a faint hint of a Slavonic accent.

Employed as a verb-deactivator (3rd class), he was noted for his rich and strange "pieces" which sometimes consisted of Beluga caviare on delicately-baked black bread, all washed down with champagne, a drink at which many of our honest artisans turned up their noses when courteously offered a glass.

His snack would be carried in a Faberge-constructed metal box on which there were representations of Peter the Great's victories, the crushing of the Decembrists and an allegory of autocracy being submitted to by peasants.

He did not stay with us long but I remember him staring sadly at dusk towards the east with just the hint of a tear in his aristocratic features. Was he, as someone suggested, Nicholas II, the Tsar of all the Russians who miraculously, with Anastasia, survived the Bolshevik massacre? Someone else said that the suggestion was purely in the realms of fantasy, but sometimes I wonder.

12

Battling Bilston

I was at Bilston Glen Colliery, Scotland's largest pit, yesterday where the adjectives flashed, the police boots crashed and the oaths went out like tracer bullets, in elegant trajectory wounding and searing sensitive spirits in the heat and testiness of industrial dispute.

I rushed in flying column to where the Press was thickest— at the gates of the embattled colliery through which a trickle of men, defying the picket lines, had gone to work earlier that day, an act that the strikers felt was one of gross provocation and deeply hurtful to coal-face solidarity. It also caused unseemly brawls between police and pickets and resulted in eight of the union's warriors being arrested on charges of obstruction, breach of the peace and resisting arrest.

Though traitors flinch and cowards fear, this column keeps the light of truth burning here and felt it incumbent to be at the dispute face where it could interview the struggling ranks of police and pickets and get, whenever necessary, the appropriate initials of those who were courteous enough to deliver such information under extreme conditions.

On Wednesday, the colliery had been the scene of Homeric struggles between the force whose lot is said not to be a happy one, and the pickets, aflame with passion, whose only interest was to tell the strike-breakers soothingly and informatively that what they were doing was extremely bad form and had probably caused Mr Scargill to shed a silent tear or so. Earlier yesterday three policemen were hurt and eight pickets arrested in clashes at the pit.

When I turned up, armed with a sawn-off notebook, four heavy-duty, picket-strength .303 HB pencils and several clips of dum-dum adjectives designed to explode on impact with the page, the scene was quiet and a little like that before the Battle of Agincourt.

Meteorologically, the day was ideal for a nice, brisk, push at the picket line—light winds, shapely cumulus clouds in a blue-grey sky, a temperature never high enough to raise emotions to extremes and the going always good to firm.

A few police had already arrived by the time I took up station with the Press corps, many of the latter strategically placed to take a sharp line of retreat through a hedge should the going became coarse and the language too rough even for their ears.

A couple of pickets were also in position, dressed a la mode in tee shirts, jeans, anoraks and matching regulation heavy boots. Some stared into the middle distance as if contemplating the coming dissolution of society in the class struggle while others uttered occasional trial mordant comments against the lads in blue as if testing them for effectiveness at short and extreme range.

At 1:20, apart from a minor scuffle between a police officer and a woman who screamed at siren pitch at him that she was a miner's wife and would not be moved from her battle place opposite the gates though all Britain's bobbies came against her, action still hung fire and Midlothian District Councillor Tom Darby, who was acutely observing the dispositions of the confrontation, took the chance of the lull to lob a cluster-bomb statement to the Press that the council was extremely concerned at the "excessive police presence" which, he claimed, exacerbated the situation and was a propaganda exercise on behalf of the management and the National Coal Board. He urged the Coal Board to resolve the situation so that Loanhead could get on with its gala day in peace, a passionate statement of priorities with which no-one felt inclined to argue.

Ten minutes later, the situation changed dramatically. A large convoy of police vehicles and Lothian Region buses driven by police, arrived, out of which broad bodies poured in a blue flood, formed themselves up in columns and marched to the picket entrance with the impressiveness of a Zulu impi on the way to attack Rorke's Drift.

At first the straggle of pickets beytrayed little interest as the opposing team fielded itself but as more policemen arrived, and formed ramparts of bodies along the roadway, miners sagged in amazement and some speculated on the crime rate that must be rising in a city and district that seemed to have been drained of all its forces of law and order.

"You never see a Bobbie in Loanhead when you want one," said an elderly citizen bitterly, "and when there's a fight, they hide behind hedges. Now you can't get moving for them.

The last assertion was correct. As far as the eye could see police filled the landscape, button bright, helmets unwavering, boots burnished and with millions of microbes being crushed under each purposeful step. It was an ideal place to ask the time and one would have expected the massed ranks to spring to attention and produce fob watches if such a request had been made.

As the hour came for the morning shift of strike-breakers to end, tension, never very high, rose a couple of notches, only to be broken by a solid phalanx of new police reinforcements marching down the road to the whistling accompaniment of miners who remembered the signature tune of the Laurel and Hardy films. Broad grins broke out on the faces of the police, answering ones came from the miners—everybody laughed. It seemed to be turning out to be a nice day and a fine, healthy, open-air life for all parties.

Up to this point, a local miner called Geordie gave his views to me and a colleague quietly and informatively, on the situation. He seemed a man of restraint and intelligence and although his views on Arthur Scargill and mine differed somewhat, I was charmed by his readiness to listen to opposing opinions.

Suddenly, he looked up and bellowed a stream of words that I found impossible to note in Pitman's shorthand and use in a family column. Red-hot adjectives linked with active verbs and fused particles hurtled from his lips. The strike-breakers were coming out and his words were directed at a cringing middle-aged man who walked eyes down, as in a bingo hall, through the police cordon.

In the distance, obscured by police bodies, each one linked with one arm coyly round the other's waist came the ritual sounds of picket chanting. Stones were thrown with more vigour than skill and the shift came out enfiladed by 25-pounder oaths, shrapnel imprecations, and warnings of what would happen to them after the strike was over, lobbing into them like hand-grenades.

There were said by the union to be only ten strike breakers but their demeanour, though understandably subdued, was unwavering. Geordie fired insults over the open sights, others did the same but the police ranks, numbering about 600, were never under any real stress against about 300 pickets, some of whom were said to have come from the West of Scotland and Larkhall, "fully tooled-up"—whatever that meant.

Then it was all over, the strike-breakers went home, perhaps for a meal and a quiet brood, and the police formed columns and marched briskly into their buses.

Suddenly, tempers flared again. A gatekeeper had inadvertently lowered the pit's gate on to the head of a passing picket causing him momentary discomfort. The crowd, deprived of the battle at the picket face, yelled insults and threats at the hapless gateman. Police about faced and ran to the scene and for one vivid moment the waves of fury on the miner's faces gave a riveting glimpse of what the day could have been. Then tempers died away, pitmen and police dispersed, and battling Bilston would no doubt live to fight another day.

13

Hard to Swallow

SOMETIMES, when I sail a yacht on the waters of Lake Windermere, deftly dodging steamers, the cable ferry, trippers' motor boats and narrowly avoiding collision with some badly-steered dinghy with a number on its bows, I reflect that these are the hallowed waters—apart from Lake Coniston—where the children in Arthur Ransome's *Swallows and Amazons* books used to beat into and run before the wind but never got the wind up, and transformed the most mundane incidents into adventures rivalling the discovery of the source of the Nile of the conquest of Everest.

The children in the novel were British in a general sense but specifically English to the backbone, loyal to family and flag, with a father an officer in the Royal Navy, a mother a product of the Australian bush, and a youngest child nick-named Vicky after a not unknown queen and empress of India.

The novels, though highly popular, were not to every child's fancy. You had to like sailing, accept the transition of ordinary people into sinister or friendly characters and places into areas of high romance such as the transformation of the highly-commercialised Bowness Bay at Lake Windermere into Rio Bay.

You had also to accept the fact that the children—John, Susan, Roger and Titty, the later female bearing a name that is hardly likely to be used in children's tales of today—were, because of the qualities of their race, articulate, enterprising, courageous, humorous and took to the sailing of small craft with the alacrity and efficiency of Nilotic crocodiles.

You knew—well, at least I knew—that with children like that, Britain and its empire would endure for at least 1,000 years the battle and the breeze since there would always be one of the bulldog breed around to tie a running bowline in an emergency or splice a frayed rope when lesser breeds without such training would fail and gnash their foreign, possibly gold-filled, teeth in frustration.

Daddy, Commander Ted Walker, RN, a man who had been about the world a bit, by and large, here and there, high and dry, and knew what was needed to keep the minds of his children alert and their bodies fighting—or at least sailing—fit, was a master of the subtle telegram sent to his family when his assent was needed for the children to go off on some adventure, there being no question of mother taking a unilateral decision.

Commander Walker would no doubt be pacing the quarterdeck with a heavy tread one dusk under the China Sea constellations and perhaps brooding on the night he was going to have at Deep Water Mary's bar in Macao when some nautical lackey would rush up and interupt his musings with a telegram from his wife asking if it was all right for the kids to sail a small boat on some British pond.

Quickly he would dash off a reply that would leave the family mildly stupefied, "Better drowned than duffers," he once wrote. "If not duffers, won't drown," and on another occasion: "Grab a chance and you won't be sorry for a might-have-been."

No simple "Yes" or "No" or even "over my waterlogged body," with him but a tendency to follow the wordiness of

Nelson's signals that caused high irritation among captains who wanted to get on with wielding the man o' war equivalent of the bicycle chain and the knuckleduster among the treacherous and gesticulating French.

Mrs Walker would no doubt run a hand over her baffled Antipodean brow and indicate to the children that she thought he meant they could go.

So they went, chin up, fully-knotted, sailing close-hauled into chapter two and beyond to the literary horizon and, one supposed, into life to pledge, I never doubted, head, heart and hand to the motherland.

I always supposed that John, the eldest, would go into the Royal Navy, command a battleship that would blow the pride of the German fleet to steely smithereens or would go down guns blazing and flag flying and still refusing iodine for his wounds under the overwhelming assault of the foe. Susan, the oldest girl, would be namely as a valorous nursing sister in the thick of any campaign, Roger would have his own command in the Merchant Navy and come through many prose-worthy scraps still playing his penny whistle and Titty I saw as a highly popular, well-formed and courageous officer in the WRNS holding her own in difficult chapters against the foe and the salty but kindly humour of male officers.

That illusion struck a rock and let in the chill deluge of reality the other day when I read in a newspaper that Ransome was said to have based the children in his books on an Anglo-Irish-Armenian family that were holidaying in Lakeland in 1929 with a boat called the *Swallow* and with whom he became friendly. One of them actually had the distinctly un-British name of Tacqui. Their surname was Altounyan.

None of them are mentioned in the story as having distinguished themselves in the late global conflict, understandable perhaps since a family with Irish and Armenian ancestry may not have had a compulsive and unswerving belief in the British imperial ethic.

I was mildly shocked to read about the main source material of the Lakeland and East Anglian tales. It was as if it had been revealed that the character of Biggles was based on a corporal in the First World War Chinese Labour Corps.

I always felt that the Walker family had a well-balanced mixture of Norse, Saxon, Norman and possibly ancient British blood in their adventurous veins, making them natural sea rovers, shanty singers, knot-tiers and winners of the last battle against any foe.

I have nothing against the Irish or Armenians and I expect there are plenty of swaggering Armenian tars adept at singing their country's version of "Rolling down to Rio" but I have never encountered them in life or literature. The thought that the Ransome characters had ancestors in that far-off Asian country many of whose inhabitants were at one time being continually massacred by the Turks, now lends an air of unreality to the tales that reason fails to eliminate.

There was in fact an air of unreality about Ransome himself. He was once, while covering the Russian civil war for the *Manchester Guardian,* said to be a member of the Petrograd Soviet, played chess with Lenin and married Evgenia—the personal secretary of Leon Trotsky—all in that order.

A newspaper reporter friend told me once how he had arrived at the Lakeland house of Mr Ransome to carry out an interview he had arranged with an author he admired greatly. He was met by an irate, red-faced, white-haired elderly man with flashing bloodshot eyes who told them to haul away sharply from his haven or he would take the wind out of my friend's sails. Taken aback, my friend fled, the reality shattering the myth.

I knew how he felt. Once, I met an elderly man who used to work on the Lakeland farm of Beatrix Potter. "She were an old devil," he said, "never seemed to like any children she met."

Disillusion comes to us all. Heave away for Armenia John, Susan etc. I'll never feel quite the same way about you again.

14

Ailing pubs

ONCE, in the dear, dead days almost beyond even my recall, I was asked by a young female cousin if I would take her into a pub—any pub—so that she could boast to her girl friends of her great daring in breaching, however temporarily, one of those many grim fortresses that upreared themselves, if not some of their customers, in the Scottish social scene and which were garrisoned largely by males.

I was not then, and am not now, an experienced pub man, but I knew at least one place where the beer was the colour of an old Stradivarius, had a thin slick of creamy foam to crown it and tasted as if drawn from some dark, deep and frosted well.

I also knew it as a place of quiet, dedicated drinking, where the decor resembled that of a condemned cell, the walls were painted the colour of old blood and the curtains, if there were any, resembled unusually heavy shrouds.

When we entered and trod softly on the sawdust-covered floor, there was the usual subdued noises characteristic of such pubs—male drinkers sighing heavily into their beer and perhaps hoping to recapture their lost innocence in the dark depths, the barman polishing the glasses with a rythmic squeak, suggestive of a child writing with a slate pencil that needed oiling, and the occasional eldritch screeches of the elderly females in the so-called "snug" or was it "jug?" bar who wore rusty bonnets, shawls of remote antiquity and cavalier decrepitude and whose faces, when occasionally smiling, resembled ruined skulls.

As we approached the bar, all noise stopped as if everyone had been felled by a mace. The male customers— all seven of them—suddenly became rigid with shock and disapproval and resembled a row of dead bats, the victims of a skilled fumigator.

The barman, a man from whom nature had removed most of the hair on his head and given him in niggardly exchange a large scalp carbuncle, gazed at my cousin with deep disapproval as Torquemada might have done if interrupted in his task of changing the minds of heretics by some representative of a local league for penal reform.

It was clear to him and to all the regulars that there was no place in that enclave of austere moral imperatives for a young girl starting out in life and clearly on her first half-pint of revelational light.

We drank up quickly and, as we left for the sinful and shameless Edinburgh streets, the noise of quiet, respectful drinking and glass polishing broke out again, like spring life returning to a countryside frozen and shocked by winter.

I mentioned this curious episode in my life only because of the television pictures shown the other day of the pub at Ross-on-Wye, Herefordshire, that became, a "time gentleman" capsule of the 1940s when its proprietor died and which was sold the other day for £45,000.

How the TV camera revived my memories of these commercial oasis of yesteryear. There were the same dark walls, the oak bar furniture, the indestructible wooden seats, and behind the bar—how times have changed—a loyal photograph of the late King George VI, to whom, I have absolutely no doubt, many a foaming tankard was raised in a health towards that monarch, the Empire in general and the Royal Family in particular.

It was—apart from the picture on the wall and the sense of unswerving support to the Royal lines which followed the Hanoverians that it gave—very like the pubs I used to know in Scotland before the juke box bellowed, chicken-in-a-basket was heard of and so-called go-go dancers went through their spasmodic movements on wet bar counters amid unwashed glasses and used potato crisp bags.

Now all is different, "changed," as the poet Yeats said, "changed utterly," and a terrible ugliness has been born in many pubs that however sparsely and even austerely furnished they may have been, were at least places where customers could, in many cases, be guaranteed a deep, almost monastic silence, in which to brood over their deep brown, beer and think deep, brown thoughts, before returning to their slate-grey lives.

That pub into which I rashly ventured with my cousin and into which I would occasionally go to make weighty if grudging conversation with the regulars, sample: "How's it going?" "You (sigh) see it all" is now a gaudy, shrieking, Gehenna of sound from over-amplified taped music of a kind that not only kills conversation but annihilates thought and serves beer that, compared with what used to be seen there in a glass darkly is gaseous, nauseous and could be described as wasp's blood.

It is now filled mainly with youths or extraordinary and violently-coloured hair styles, all talking at the tops of their voices to make themselves heard above the boom of the loudspeakers, the equivalent in decibel-rating, I imagine, of the British artillery barrage that heralded the start of the battle of El Alamein. It is no longer a place for the enjoyment of a quiet, still pint over which to contemplate the riddle of the universe or ponder philosophically on the crimes, follies and misfortunes of mankind and how, if fate would only stay neutral, he (the customer) might stand half a chance in life.

For someone like myself, who might occasionally want a half-pint of faintly alcoholic petro-chemical muck, humorously dubbed beer, and a chance to think his own thoughts or talk to some knowledgeable chap on a topic of mutual interest like Roman naval construction in the reign of the Emperor Trajan or the development of Romanian peasant dress from 1688 to 1912, traditional pubs are becoming ar rare as snowflakes in the Sahara.

I read in a newspaper recently that because of a slump in business—caused by more people drinking less in pubs or drinking unsociably at home, or in wine or cocktail bars, and the popularity of home brewing and inexpensive beer in super markets—pubs are having to change themselves out of all recognition in a bid to attract customers.

That report sends a deep chill to my stomach like certain kinds of lager. How far will these metamorphoses have to go before pub owners decide they are successful enough to bring back customers in their former numbers for the slake of their thirsts?

I have seen changes that were not only almost beyond belief but would also have beggared my description had I not had in my possession a decent number of adjectives laid by for just such days of pouring gloom. Full many a glorious tavern have I seen flatter the customer with sovereign beer, gilding pale glasses with heavenly alchemy, anon permit the basest changes to be made and from the forlorn world its traditional visage hide and show the alien face of an Iberian fishing village, its muttering lackeys disguised as fishermen, or as a Corsican bandit's lair, the staff dressed in original ethnic garb and muttering to themselves in local demotic.

I wish I had as many pints, or at least the money to buy them, for the pubs I have seen become transformed into something strange, if not always rich, lurid with multi-coloured lights resembling a spaceship out of the film *Close Encounters* or become transported back into Elizabethan days with plastic oak beams, reproduction swords and halberds on the wall and bar-maids bosomed and buttressed for the part, dispensing with accuracy foaming tankards of highly-expensive alcoholic sludge that would, in the days of good Queen Bess, have had mine host run through with a light laugh or strange oath.

I believe that people are fleeing from many pubs—there are still some good ones around, I do not dispute that—because they cannot stand the sound of them and the sights, resembling some noisy circle in Dante's *Inferno*, that they see there.

In my necessarily-biased opinion the masses will not—at least the middle-aged ones—return in their old numbers until they can go down to a place again of the lonely pint and the pie and where all they ask is a tall glass and enough light to steer it by, with the whisky's kick and the reveller's song and a joke-telling bore, and a quiet brood and a dreamless sleep when the long drink's o'er.

15

Mother takes a lesson in Chess

NOW, I don't want you to shout at me. After all, I am your mother and I am entitled to some respect and I did teach you to play snakes and ladders when you were small—and heavens knows you weren't too bright at it. Remember, I'm only trying to play chess with you because the doctor said you should have your mind occupied while you are convalescing and it's important not to use your voice too much.

Yes dear, you've explained the moves beautifully—no son could have done more for a mother—and there's no need to go over them for the 23rd time. Couldn't we just play now? Do I know the object of the game? Oh, no, I didn't realise there was one. I thought you just kept knocking off all the little men—like in draughts—until there were no more left.

Hmm; I see. Well, it sounds a bit complicated, but I've no doubt I'll pick it up as we go along. Do let's play now; I'm dying to move these pieces.

Isn't this lovely? You moving your men and me moving mine. Such a quiet, restful game and so good for the mind too. I feel awfully intellectual.

Ah ha! I'm going to move my pawn–there. Is that good? No, I know you're not supposed to tell me, but I thought you might give me just a little hint. Oh, you've moved that pretty horse thing out. Well, my friend, I'll move out this little pawn. No, I don't know why I did that. No, I can't give a reason. No, I can't see any danger. Yes, I know I've got to

think out every move. Look here what have I done wrong?
Why are you tormenting me like this? You say you're going
to teach me a lesson and take my pawn. Well, that's not fair;
I'm only learning you know. After all, you can't expect a
woman of my age to pick up a game like this in a day. I bet
I've picked it up quicker than some of those girl friends of
yours would have done. Honestly, some of them look as if
Snap would crack their minds with the effort.

All right, all right, I'll concentrate on the game. I'm going
to move my queen into that square. Oh, the queen doesn't
jump over the other pieces. Well, you never told me that.
No, you never. Pardon me . . . Well, if you did, I never heard
you.

Very well, I've put the queen back. It's on the wrong
square you say. That was the very square I took it from. I
swear to heaven it was. Look here, there's no need to shout.
I know you're 35 and not a child any longer, but I don't
think that entitles you to go on like that. I tell you it was a
genuine mistake.

Just settle down and please I'll make my next move. Ah
ha! I can take this bishop . . . so? Oh, I've taken one of my
own men. Yes, I know I can't do that. Of course, I know it
was foolish. Well, I just wasn't thinking. Honestly, the way
you carry on—you'll never get back to work at this
rate.

Heigh ho, it's a long game, the chess. You need to have a
keen, analytical mind for it. Not like mine, I'm afraid—or
yours for that matter. I don't want to hurry you son, but I
wish you'd get a move on; you've been sitting there
motionless for half and hour, and I want to make you some
gruel soon.

Now please keep your voice down. I didn't realise it was

my move all this time. Really, if you're going to be so irritable, I'm just not going to play with you again.

All right, I'll make my move now. There, I've moved that piece. The knight doesn't move like a bishop! No, I know that, I swear I thought it was a bishop. Well, it looked like a bishop from where I'm sitting.

No, there's no need for me to get my spectacles, I can see perfectly well. I'll move this piece, then. All right, allright, all right I'm sorry—that's one of your pieces. Please don't get so flushed—I wonder if I should take your temperature again. Look, son, I've moved the king. Oh, the king only moves one square at a time. Don't tell me, I've put it back on the wrong square again.

Look, don't scream, I'll move this castle. No, I won't, yes I will. Should I? Well, you might help me a bit.

No. I honestly don't know what I'm doing. I'm not feeling well and I'm getting dizzy. What's this? You say I've got a pawn in my hand. No I haven't. Oh yes I have. All right, I'll put it back. I can't remember what square it came from—can you?

Look, I'm getting awfully mixed up; I don't think women ought to play chess. Well, I can't help it if I keep moving my pieces then taking them back again—I'm nervous. Oh. now look what you've made me do—I've knocked over the board and upset the pieces.

All right my dear, don't cry. Keep perfectly quiet and I'll mix you a mild sedative. Later, if you like, we can have a game of snakes and ladders. You'd like that, wouldn't you? After all, what's a mother for if she can't help her son.

16

Not known: return to Zenda

NOTHING much in this world surprises me now but occasionally I do get a jolt that still disturbs my massive phlegm and makes my eyebrows rise with a faint interrogative or alarmed movement.

I was jolted badly the other day when in a bookshop of apparent repute not 100 miles from this office I approached a young female assistant staring into space with the concentrated scrutiny of the Lady of the Shallot gazing into her mirror. Seeking a gift for a young friend in the shape of a book I had savoured in my early youth, I asked the girl if the establishment stocked "The Prisoner of Zenda." by Anthony Hope.

A baffled frown flickered across her features. "Is it new?" she asked. With a heavy sigh of one who suddenly feels he has read too long and too much, I told her the novel was first published in 1894, was now a minor English classic and that Hollywood—recognising the box-office appeal—had made three films based on its plot.

Disbelief lingered in her eyes. "Never heard of it", she said dismissively, her words seeming to indicate that the book therefore could never have existed. Consenting, however, to gratify the bizarre whim of a customer she looked up the title in a booklist and with an air of triumph told me that the novel was out of print.

Never heard of Castle Zenda and its royal prisoner! Surprise gave way to pity for a wretched child who would probably get married, have children, get divorced and remarried, etc., without ever having known and presumably wanting to know, about a book that might have made her young blood dance and tingle and brought the petal-pink flush of excitement to her cheeks, thus enabling her to economise on make-up.

The book may be in a publishing limbo but for me, the image of Ruritania, that obscurely-placed kingdom in Central Europe, where citizens were always running each other through the heart with swords to the accompaniment of mocking laughter, will forever be sharply imprinted in my mind.

What is the picture I get on the Zenda cerebral channel? It is of course a moonlight scene, the air quivering with tension and romance in which all good people not directly connected with the chapters are firmly out of sight. There are horsemen galloping through the pine-scented forests out to do or foil dirty work against the royal family of Elphberg and the rightful possessor of the crown.

Somewhere on castle battlements, there is the jolly clink of steel meeting steel and—as in the film versions—there are gentlemanly conversations between the combinatants as the blades flash and the swordsmen progress into the main hall where in strict rotation, tapestries will be slashed, candles will be sliced through with resultant comment: "Very clever but not I think (clink, clank, tinkle) . . . clever enough," before the villian is dispatched and falls dramatically into the moat with a howl of despair loud enough to make the lice leap off the castle guards.

There will be secret trysts in summer-houses and hunting-lodges. A handsome, tautly muscled, lean-as-a-lance Englishman with noble connections and a manly hand-shake will do what all Englishmen of his class and inclination did at that time—right wrongs, keep his morals and sword blade clean and pluck bright honour from the pale pages by giving up the woman of his choice and a throne and disappear over the literary horizon.

There has been a correspondence in the "Times" for some weeks now in which readers have speculated on the exact geographical location of Ruritania, placing it in Austria, Romania, Bavaria or Czechoslovakia. I myself am persuaded that it was situated near the latter country. Certainly the inhabitants all hiss, whisper or threaten in German but there is also a distinct Slavonic element shown in some of the names of the characters especially that of its distinguished military leader Marshall Strakencz.

To me its place on the map matters less than its fate today. With its distinct Teutonic leanings, it would, I suspect, have sided with Germany and Austria in the First World War and come under the Nazi jackboot in 1939, the monarchy which up till then had continued with unabated popularity, fleeing to the safety of well-known publishing houses in America.

Liberated by the Soviet hordes, its tenderness for free and often desperate enterprise and its cottage conspiracy industry brutally subdued, the country became part of the Communist bloc and a signatory of the Warsaw Pact, its main industry the production of cloaks and daggers to international political subverts.

Visitors to Ruritania now would see some of the stately homes of the former noblesse transformed into rest and recreation centres for the workers, the great cathedral in Streslau now an anti-religious museum and the castle at Zenda turned into a medieval banqueting hall, the guests served by full-bosomed proletarian wenches in traditional

Left-wing costume.

But at night, despite the flag of revolution fluttering on the places of power, the heavily-armed police patrols and the massive ferro-concrete statue of Lenin in the market place, the sound of ghostly horses' hooves can sometimes be heard and the specital figures of swordsmen, film producers and extras can be seen fleetingly inducing superstitious awe into the most rational Marxist.

Conspiracy is in the very air the people breathe. One day the king will come back to his own. Ruritania of the mind, despite the ignorance of bookshop assistants, still lives.

17

The clockwork civil servants

TELEPHONE calls to the Post Office speaking clock by civil servants at New St Andrew's House and Chesser House, where a total of 2000 are employed, were made at a rate of 1000 a week, a monitoring machine has disclosed. Apart from time calls a high number of civil servants made use of such other telephone information services as cricket scores, recipes, weather and tourist advice.

"At the third stroke," announced the woman in ringing tones for the record, "it will be 10.37 and 15 seconds." Miss Julie Penworthy, executive officer, late of Ag and Fish, Min of Def and Dep of Env, felt her cheeks suffuse sealing-wax-pink with deep pleasure as she laid down her phone with a quietly efficient wrist-flick that was the envy of less deft colleagues. The third successive time check that morning, the thirty-seventh that week, the 5321st—according to her careful notes—that year and still, incredibly, the experience seemed ever new, always thrilling and always able to fill her with a sense of achievement and well-being.

With quiet triumph she announced the discovery to her colleagues. An immediate ripple of interest moved across the room where facts were normally sucked up by the occupants like household fluff in a vacuum cleaner, but any that brought news of the steady approach of retirement day on an index-related pension was received with the kind of reverent joy a puppy of acknowledged dental ability reserves for an unbitten ankle.

86

Even old McBracken, who was once Mr Big in denaturing of wheat statistics for the Home Counties in 1952, a tweed-suited, tobacco-stained, statistic-calloused desk warrior who had been making heavy weather trying to understand a poem in Welsh from Cardiff which he had dialled in the mistaken belief that he had been on to the weather forecast for South Hants and Isle of Wight (including the coast area between Poole Harbour and Chichester), an area about which he knew little and cared less, was visibly impressed.

"Phew," he whistled appreciatively, between his finely chiselled bureaucratic teeth with wide margins between and Official Secrets Act tightened lips: "That's good. I can remember when it was only 9.32 and four seconds although it seems less than 30 minutes and five seconds ago at the third stroke."

Miss Penworthy flushed even more deeply at what Rudyard Kipling had rated the highest praise that could be offered—that between colleague and colleague. She looked around the room warmly, a feeling partly caused by emotion and partly by the fourth cup of tea a low-grade office worker had brought her that morning.

It was a stirring sight and made nonsense of the canard whipped up by envious breeds outside the corridors and can teens of power that civil servants had a morbid dread of hard work and were about as active as two-toed sloths unless continually primed with tea and strong biscuits. There, for instance, in the corner, with a face like a crumpled Easter Island statue, was young Jeremy Stapler, head down, "phone up", amassing vital information on the main events of the day in and around London in Spanish.

Nearby was old George Buckpasser, 40 years in the Civil Service game and still only a clerical officer but an old dear who would never stab you in the back if he could let fly at you from the front. He was up to his steadfast ears tapping the phone service gardening information with hardly ever a complaint on his loyal lips. Beside him, wearing a regulation clerical assistant frown and matching steel wool cardigan, was Miss Betsy Bundrop (Business New Summary and "Financial Times" Index phoner) and who was, it was rumoured, being groomed for executive officer stardom and a chance to dial the coveted cricket scores in season as well as the daily recipe.

Miss Penworthy could remember a time (at the third stroke 11.57 and eight seconds precisely) when she had met her first real live Civil Service principal. She was then a simple lass with only her regulation marriage dowry in mind whose pink little delicate index-related finger hardly had the strength to dial a bedtime story let alone crook it to summon a panting and eager acolyte to fetch her a butter biscuit and a cup of tea, milk without, from the canteen.

The principal, a man gone grey and finger-worn in the big-time phone service in the Min. of Inf., revealed to her the benefits of Civil Service life. "If you work hard the rewards will be commensurate with one of a superior skill in an organisation which in many respects is like a giant exclusive club. You may start off as a clerical assistant or lowly typist getting the bread and butter stuff about ski-ing conditions at the principal Scottish centres but if you apply yourself there is no prize that will not be open to you when you reach executive officr status—the Test Match scores, maybe even (here he looked hard at her to see if the glittering prospects had made her show weakness unbecoming in an elite group), the mighty speaking clock itself."

It had not been an easy climb and some people she knew

had fallen by the way. Not long ago, a 27-year old civil servant had been dismissed from his job in the Cabinet Office where he treacherously claimed he had not enough to do and had obtained evening and weekend work in a restaurant cooking hamburgers.

There had obviously been no-one to show him how to get weather forecasts, say from the Cardiff area, the food prices news and, if he had used the head, the motoring information from Scotland which also covered the main routes into England.

Beside her lay a list of statistics relating to butter subsidies claimed in Britain in 1971 which she was asked to compile—she suspected a joke—for the top brass, many of whom were known to have a keen sense of humour. Meanwhile she had her duty to perform. "And eight seconds," said the voice caught unawares.

Miss Penworthy sighed happily. All was going as well as a good civil servant could wish. "Like clockwork," old McBracken commented approvingly—and he was right.

18

Revealing a jungle secret

I T was perhaps fitting that in a previously married life, apparently rich in verbal tooth and claw, the Burtons should have become reunited in a village deep in the Botswana bush. According to a report in the "Times," only two people witnessed the wedding and afterwards no-one but a pair of interested hippos and a rhino watched—from a safe distance—the couple drinking champagne at a river bank.

In fact, in the background and perhaps even unnoticed by the stars in their erratic marital courses were three other prominent local inhabitants, according to this column's African Affairs correspondent, Geoffrey Krakatoa. Sources close to the Nile, Limpopo and Tugela and other prominant rivers reported the unexpected appearance of a Mr Fred Tarzan, his wife, Jane, and a middle-aged gentleman called "Boy".

Now in her sixties, Mrs Tarzan still has a gracious gamin-type beauty enhanced by the moist air of the jungle though small shadows play occasionally about her eyes. Her hair, expertly blue-rinsed as a charming concession to a civilisation which she so dramatically abjured when she met Mr Tarzan in a sensational romantic encounter on a then fashionable branch in 1936, she maintains an elegant simplicity of manner combined with a childlike wonder which touched the heart of man, ape, soldier-ant, tree tick and bull elephant in many of the better-class jungles.

Mr Tarzan himself—he adopted the name "Fred" in

1963 in deference to a final British colonial Government census before the country received independence—is still straight-backed and distinguished-looking though in his seventies but has, alas, still not managed to overcome the intricacies of the English language beyond simple sentences of not more than four words, not all of which necessarily make sense though Jane claims he understands every word she says to him.

Strangely enough there is no record of the couple ever having married and for many acquainted with the life of this strange family, the arrival of a male boy, named with endearing simplicity, "Boy," for a time seemed to confuse the issue. The baby came as a result of an accident—a plane one in the jungle of which he was the sole survivor. Brought into the Tarzan household, he was able in a surprisingly short time to speak idiomatic American, fluent enough to delight the ear of the most discerning rascally Transatlantic trader.

Though witnesses at the jungle wedding it was unlikely that this ceremony would be emulated by Fred and Jane. There was no trace of bitterness in Jane's eyes as she watched the elegant champagne bottle float symbolically down the river, mingling romantically with hippos, drifting crocodiles and local native beer cans. "Mr Tarzan," she said. "will get round to asking me one day when he has mastered forming the question. Till then I am content to wait."

How have the Tarzans fared in new, developing, de-mythologised Africa? Naturally there have been changes. Their tree-tops home is now a five-star restaurant, visited by the uncrowned heads of Africa and the cream of local society where rich organic Afro-European dishes are made under the expert supervision of Jane. Branches are expected to be established elsewhere. "Boy," now a lad in his late forties still goes on routine tree-swinging patrol, mainly for the benefit of tourists, and appears regularly on Radio Afrodasia in a programme entitled "Woodland Ways".

Fred Tarzan, now too old even to swing from any but the lowest creeper tends to wander about dejected staring aggressively into the averted eyes of passing lions and crocodiles. He often appears at El Garish University, at the invitation of the Government chief psychiatric adviser, where his descriptions of jungle life continually fascinate.

Meanwhile, what of Chita the chimp? He was last heard of in Beverley Hills, California where in 1969 he had become the popular owner of a tavern and where his racy anecdotes of the home life of the Tarzans never failed to amuse customers. Good luck to them all.

19

Snuff and nonsense

ABOUT 500 million years ago when I was young I had an aunt who kept a newsagent and tobacconist shop. Its main characteristic was a delicious smell of the nicotinal delights that attracted hundreds of devotees of the weed daily to the premises to buy products ranging from Woodbine—it was "Wild" then and its commercial image was equated with that of the cloth-capped worker about to start on a hunger march or wait his turn in the dole queue—to a fag called De Reszke which had a picture of a monocled major on the packet and was smoked by the aspiring-to-elegant bourgeoisie and the upper-lower middle classes who liked to feel they were at a common puff with the masses.

I used to stand in that shop and inhale delightedly the atmosphere of rich Turkish tobacco, as smoked in cigarettes by Egyptian soldiers, perhaps under Gordon of Khartoum, wearing fezes and pointing rifles into the middle desert distance. Mingled with that odour was the distinctive reek of Navy Cut Plug, a tobacco that lay coiled in tins like black cobras and which were charmed out by my aunt's businesslike hand and then sliced into portions for elderly pipe smokers with faces the colour of old kippers.

I can see them now, the cigarette smokers, coughing and wheezing in their smokey ardour to get at the temporary illusion of life-enhancement, sometimes indulgently offering me the cigarette cards of "Miracles of Pond Life," "Famous British Poisoners," or "Air Raid Precautions"—one of the

latter series showing a delicately-boned British lass working
a fragile-looking stirrup pump in the general direction of a
small, genteely-smoking incendiary bomb—or curtly
"buzz-off"-ing my pleas for additions to my collection as
they claimed they were saving up the cards for their own
offspring.

The pipe smokers were—as might be expected—stolid-
looking men with far-away looks in their eyes, some
resembling the young J.B. Priestley, who spoke between
puffs and lighting-up noises like "mmmppfff, mmmmppfff"
about the merits of Latakia, Perique or Virginia tobaccos,
or exotic mixtures containing them, and would produce
pouches to be filled up resembling pieces of ancient elephant
hide or Egyptian mummy's skin.

Cigar smokers were also in evidence although in the
minority of the customer total and were mainly, according
to the lurid impressionist images of my childhood memory,
commercial travellers with sleekly-plastered hair, toothbrush
moustaches and ingratiating smiles that fell like water off
my aunt's small, rigid and unimpressionable back. A
woman wise and wary in the ways of commercial wiles, she
could dismiss over-zealous salesmen with the dread ukase:
"Come back next week when I'm not so busy," which was
the shop-keeper equivalent of sentencing someone to the
electric chair.

The most curious of her customers, however, was a group
of ancient men and women who used to drift in furtively like
wraiths and were charcterised by a distinctive sharp smell
that hit other customers like assegai thrusts up the nostrils.
One of them, an old Irish woman with a face like the relief
map of MacGillycuddy's Reeks and wearing a dark-brown
shawl and rust-coloured bonnet, used to lean familiarly

over the counter—and while my aunt recoiled and stood as if pinned to the rows of Gold Flake, Black Cat and Piccadilly fags on the wall—would ask hoarsely for a couple of ounces of Kendal Brown.

She was, of course, a snuff-sniffer, hooked hopelessly and happily on the old powder, her life a delicious sniff and sneeze, an olfactory Elysium and her ways shrouded in a mist of the stuff, which, if anyone was as incautious as to pat her on the back, would rise up in the air thickly like a miasma from the fever-ridden Florida Everglades and make those around gasp, splutter and weep surprised tears from stinging eyes.

Once, the old girl, emerging from a delirium of sneezes that made the "Red Letter," "Family Star," and "My Weekly" magazines flutter their pages like aspen leaves, offered me a sample sniff from her precious powder supply which she placed on the back of her talon-like hand. Hesitantly I did so and purely to satisfy my emerging spirit of scientific curiosity. In an instant my whole being seemed to shatter in a sneeze that was like a gas explosion. The old dear let out an eldritch screech as the gaiety of the situation overcame her and when I emerged from the trauma, red-faced and weeping, I vowed, although I was only ten, that I would never be tempted by a woman again, at least, I amended, not by snuff-bearing ones.

There are, it is estimated, about half a million snuff-takers in Britain, 40 per cent of whom are women, who believe that the human nose and snuff go together like bacon and eggs, cream and coffee, Marks and Spencer, Morecambe and Wise.

Some people claim that the real snuff-taker does not sneeze but I feel that if this is not the final orgiastic act resulting from dipping one's nose into the powder, what other delight is left to the snuffer apart from the dubious one of merely snuffing the nostrils full of brown powder.

According to a Press report snuff may become cheaper thanks to a tax cut originating from the Common Market. With the abolition of snuff duty the British Government will not be imposing a direct revenue levy on a tobacco product for the first time since an impost was put on in 1590.

A friend who is practically covered in snuff pointed out that the best way to cure a cold that I have was to take a quick sniff. "Clears your head in no time," he assured me.

For the first time in all these years I weakened. My nose twitched expectantly and I placed my reddened nostrils on a snuff sample. Once more my body twitched as if an electric current had been passed through it and I sneezed with the force of a salvo of 15-inch guns. My cold is still however with me and I have to tell snuff-takers that I can get more explosive and sensual sneezes as a result of streptococci microbes than anything sold out of a tin; my way is Nature's way and—excuse me while I sneeze—I intend to stick to it.

20

Spy house of August Moon

OF the hundreds of Chinese restaurants throughout Britain at least 15 percent are used as part of the intelligence network and listening posts of the Chinese Government, according to "A History of the Chinese Secret Service." by Richard Deacon, historical writer and former foreign manager of the "Sunday Times".

"Boiled or flied lice?" The question, hissed through the thin, cruel Asiatic lips of the waiter with the livid scar stretching from under the ear lobe to the base of the chin jolted Harr Thursday, known in the British Government's counter Chinese restaurant espionage branch as Agent X, into a state of nerve-pounding alertness.

There was something chillingly familiar about the man. What was it? Could it be the sinister pock-marks on his face, the mirthless grin with which he had handed him the Egg Foo Yong-stained menu and the cryptically-significant way he had asked: "Hello squire, you eat Chinese or English?"

There was also the disturbing way he had of plucking at the left sleeve of his waiter's jacket that spoke either of extreme nervous tension or was a gesture to reassure himself that a billpad or weapon or both lay concealed there.

Where had he seen the man before? Was it in the Golden Flea restaurant in sun-drenched, palm-greased, tourist-soaked Balik Papan where little Miss Suey, the sloe-eyed quick-moving Eurasian agent had got the chop between the chicken noodle soup and the lychees, or was it as the inscrutable chauffeur of the expressionless ambassador of a traditionally secretive large Oriental Power or even—and Thursday shivered at the thought—as the lone occupant of a windowless, air-conditioned office with the name "T.J. Fudlow Associates" known only to a few and situated high on a tower block building near London's Hyde Park?

Were they on to him? Thursday was a real pro—tough, unscrupulous, a loner but the anxiety lines deepened on his face as the waiter's eyes stared at him in what seemed fathomless malevolence at being kept waiting for an order.

"Er . . ." he replied with unaccustomed nervousness, "fried rice please," and he paused significantly, "China tea to follow." The waiter grunted acknowledgement and turned away whispering something to another Oriental clad in faultless evening wear who had earlier been regarding Thursday with an unblinking stare through a crack in a bamboo curtain.

Thursday toyed uncomfortably with a paper napkin on which was printed a representation of the willow pattern, and to take his mind off the feeling of impending doom, emphasised by his hackles rising slowly like a cobras from a basket, he recalled sinister affairs connected with other Chinese restaurants such as the obscure one at a certain naval dockyard named 'Wan Sik Blok," where young Ronnie Carstairs, one of the brightest chaps in the espionage game, had come to grief. It was rumoured that he had been offered as an extra dish, a plate of 3000-year-old bird's nest soup and after a few timid sips had turned green and rushed staggering into the open air. After an ominous splash was heard, he was never seen again.

Then there was Blake, a veteran at the Chinese restaurant caper, who had stopped the drainage secrets of Glasgow being sent to the Mao Government. He was given an orange by an old mandarin at a Chinese restaurant in Scotland near a high-quality depth-charge factory and his mind afterwards went as soft as noodles in sweet and sour pork soup.

"May I sit down?" Thursday's stomach lurched like soup spilled by a waiter as a ravishing blonde female sat beside him. Was she . . .? There was something about the way pieces of chicken chow mein still clung to her superbly-tailored suit that screamed of danger. Perhaps he was getting old. This was a dangerous game and but for the free food he would have packed it in long ago.

"Certainly," he said and rose in a display of a chivalry now unfortunately dying out. There was a click and suddenly he found himself looking at a bamboo shoot held in a very steady hand. At the same time a bread roll was thrust painfully into his back. He had fallen for the oldest trick of all. In the kitchen the dread King Prawn gave a dreadful chuckle. Suddenly for Thursday all was blackness. Now read on.

21

Musical Goliath goes to war

AS a long-forgotten scent, snatch of half-remembered music or a sound—such as the slow, metallic grind of tramcars heard in Blackpool, that unexpected outpost of transport civilisation—can evoke memories long cobwebbed in dark cupboards of the mind, so can a word suddenly repaint in pristine colours a section of one's life, long buried under the mental detritus of the decades.

Such a word appeared on a newspaper page yesterday. "Wurlitzer." Ah, how the name brings back for me the period a few years before the Second World War and for a few years after Mr Chamberlain's curiously flat and spirit-depressing declaration of hostilities, when the streets of Edinburgh suddenly started to smell of wet sandbags, and back greens and gardens were dug up to house air-raid shelters and when Vera Lynn as good as promised as a war aim bluebirds over the white cliffs of Dover and millions of voices chorused one of the most depressing patriotic songs ever written: "There'll always be an England."

A Wurlitzer is not, as might be imagined, a native of a small German state but a species of super-impressive cinema organ. Looking to the layman's awed eye as if it were made of battleship steel, cast iron, brass, chromium, teak and mahogany, it was designed to rise and descend through the cinema floor, all notes blazing like a brisk destroyer action at Jutland, and which had the near-miraculous effect of making interval audiences pause momentarily in their tasks of grinding through their toffees and demolishing with rythmic precision their ice-creams and box-rustling chocolates.

According to a Press report, a Wurlitzer organ which used to entertain audiences at Manchester's Odeon cinema has now been housed in the Free Trade Hall and an inaugural concert was held to mark the transfer of the 35-ton instrument to its new home.

A few other Wurlitzers are apparently still booming throughout the country, most taken from cinemas and housed in private homes—one owner still has his going up and down through the floor to get the best effect out of it—and plans are in hand and afoot to set up a museum to house Wurlitzeriana.

I was first introduced to the impact of this musical Goliath as a small child when Edinburgh's Odeon was, in a fit of hot patriotic pride, called the New Victoria. Suddenly, without any real warning, during the period between the Movietone News and a trailer on the latest Deanna Durbin film, the "mighty Wurlitzer" as it was called with suitable respect for its Wagnerian sonic powers, rose through the floor like a caged beast suddenly unleashed and began to crash out a melody that I recognised after I had taken my hands from my ears as "Some Day My Prince Will Come"—but which to those in the front stalls must have had a distinct resemblance to the sound that might have been made had the Scott Monument fallen on the glass roof of the Waverley Station.

Along with it came a pleasant-faced young man (called Richard Telfer), clad in faultless evening wear, who appeared not so much to be playing an instrument as tackling it in the same way as a lion tamer would cautiously poke a chair and whip at a somewhat short-tempered lion.

His skill was obviously very great and he managed to make the instrument sound like Shangri-la doves in the film "Lost Horizon" or by popular request, thunder like the trump of doom in some portentous melody.

As he coaxed soft and sonorous effects out of the instrument, spotlights played on the organ giving the player a faintly Mephistophelian appearance and when he disappeared into the depths one could faintly hear him working in the earth to subdue the instrument as it thundered its defiance of "I Do Like To Be By The Seaside."

I remember when Mr Telfer appeared in uniform and announced that he had been called to the colours. The audience stood up and cheered. This was clearly war *a outrance* and was appreciated as such.

For a time the Wurlitzer fell silent and the guns began to boom a sound that eclipsed even the mightiest efforts of that organ. Later, however, Mr Telfer was able to return to the cinema from time to time and did much to boost morale by getting audiences to join in choruses, the words of which were flashed onto the screen and which had a little ping-pong ball apparently bouncing on each word to keep people in time to the music.

It was a time when people were encouraged to be matey with each other and at one such session with the Wurlitzer, people were exhorted to shake hands with their nearest neighbours, something unheard of in an Edinburgh cinema until then. I remember offering my pink, sweet-stained fingers to a dignified Edinburgh woman who looked as if she might not be able to bear the terrible effects of total war much longer.

Down in London and on the Clyde, the bombs were dropping and in Edinburgh and in other organ-fortunate cities, the Wurlitzers were booming their own defiance. It was quite a noisy period. I expect most people my age will remember it as such.

Out in the dark Edinburgh street people groped hesitantly in the black-out, and occasionally searchlights swept the skies like those in 20th Century Fox films criss-crossing above a futuristic city.

Inside the cinemas, audiences now flecked with uniforms were watching the curves coyly appearing from a Rita Hayworth negligee or hearing the frenzied, confident tones of a news commentator saying that the Germans would never break through the Maginot Line and that the French Army (appropriate shots of grinning poilus marching to the Front) was the most powerful military machine in the world and would make Hitler flinch when he was matched against French steel.

Outside, the billboards announced: "Paris Falls" and "BEF return to France" and for the first time a feeling of scepticism, bordering on disbelief, made itself felt towards such blatant propagandist efforts.

Then came the interval and up rose the theatre organ, brave as a battle ensign of a warship, with its dedicated player grappling with the controls and the audience felt that whatever happened we had got the mighty Wurlitzer and the Germans had not.

I rejoice that some of these spectacular instruments still survive. In a sense they were a secret weapon that Hitler with all his cunning did not reckon with. Thank you mighty melodic Wurlitzer and that you Mr Telfer.

22

Fracula and Drankenstein

OF course I have been watching the late-night horror films on television. Hasn't everybody? When I peer into the Gothic gloom of my screen, all the cares and grossness of the age, the slings and pea-shots of outrageous misfortune, slip from my mind and I realise with the thin, crescent grin—the precise shape of the blade in "The Pit and the Pendulum"—that by the big, broad, box-like forehead of an identikit, hand-built, grunting, strangling monster that some people could be worse off than I am.

I was, in a sense, reared on a rich diet or horror from early childhood, being sent by my relief-sighing parents into the carbolic-soap scented gloom of Saturday matinee picture houses to have my spine chilled, blood frozen and hair raised aloft with other eye-popping, jaw-bulging-with-furniture-glue-toffee children.

I must have given the peaks of at least a dozen school caps of mine serrated edges as I chewed them in a frenzy of nervous oral gratification while Dracula, dressed immaculately for dinner, slid as if on castors out of his sarcophagus.

I got to know the characters like the front of my foot—mad scientists, heroines with 18-carat hearts and one-carat minds and sometimes equipped with mammalian protuberances that would bring a weak gleam of interest into rheumy eyes of some sinister old servant of the local vampire who would tell guests to the castle: "Walk this way"—a difficult feat since the old lad looked and moved like a gnarled, moss-covered-on-the-north-side tree-trunk with legs.

Sometimes the characters would merge into each other in my over-stimulated imagination and I would envisage in my darkest dreams of ancient Hollywood crypts and secret laboratories, a hand-made vampire called Fracula, a character I would invariably confuse with a similar mis-shapen, pale-faced, shark-toothed, elegantly-dressed chappie called Drankenstein.

Watching the repeats of these creaking, line-streaked old films—some of which were made with superb style and conviction—as well as the blood-stained, wolf-flecked, bat-squeaking, monster-haunting, heroine-shrieking Hammer Films productions, I saw as in the front stalls darkly all the dear old characters that I had come to know and dread rise before me: they would gesticulate and jerk through their parts and disappear into the swirling mists of phantom-haunted memory only to be resurrected when the next series of repeats appears, probably in six months time.

To those who are unfamiliar with monster, mad scientists and vampire territory, herewith a brief but I believe comprehensive guide to the countryside and inhabitants.

Manservants: Invariably sinister, sometimes with hunchbags under their squinting eyes, given to playing melancholy tunes on a lute while the young master is either at the drawing board muttering: "I'm sure I've got it right this time." or having a quick bite and drink with an unsuspecting guest. Generally answers to the name "Igor" and will work like a beaver if allowed to cringe, cower and leer and lope to his black (heh:heh:) heart's content.

Hero: Young friend of mad scientist or non-paying guest at Castle Dracula. Often wears dear-stalker hat and matching bemused look. Built to arrive in time's nick and have hair-breadth escapes rescuing the heroine from being turned into a museum waxwork or from having the juices of 20,000 lobsters injected into her in the belief—probably mistaken—that it will turn her into a lobster, he is available for a final embrace with the lady while the monster is being lightly barbecued in a burning building and vampire-hunters claim their stake in Dracula's elegant shirt-front.

Heroine: Sometimes daughter of mad scientist, sometimes wife, who is invariably in receipt of a phrase like: "Martha, I told you never to come into this room." Although scarcely equipped to deal with your well-set inquisitive and short-tempered patchwork horror in the attic or cellar, generally finds her way into the forbidden area where she is given to screaming musically as a robot-like hand lands heavily on her shapely, sloping shoulders.

Peasants: Either merry-making—in a triumph of hope over experiment—to celebrate the arrival of the third generation of the Frankenstein family into their midst or fleeing in terror as someone spots a light in an upstairs room of Dracula's castle. Given to telling visitors "No-one but a fool would be out on a Walpurgis Nacht while they are in this part of Transylvania," or staring sullenly at visitors who have asked them: "What is everyone afraid of? Why don't you speak? Are you all deaf as well as dumb?"

Police chief: Wears a uniform that is a cross between that of a Uhlan and a Ruritanian rear-admiral. Sometimes has an eye patch and a metallic arm which, with his good hand, is brought to the salute, hand-shake or posture of defence or surrender, but which sometimes tends to go badly awry.

Has a melancholy and somewhat sardonic look as if he has seen bad times and expects to see a lot worse and wouldn't be in the fuzz business if it wasn't for the free uniform, all the adrenalin-raising he wants, and the cash.

Often says: "Ah, Herr Englander. I could tell you a story about how I got ziss arm ven ze first Dr Frankenstein here was . . ."

Todays weather and meteorological outlook: Wide patches of mist and fog over low ground. Rain with gale-force winds before evening with thunder and lightning probable as Dr Frankenstein throws the final switch to solve the riddle of the universe and jerk the monster into a hard shoe shuffle, or Count Dracula tells his guest: "I hope sincerely that you will be very happy here and stay for a long time. Sleep well."

Castle Dracula: Heating, plumbing and decor reminiscent of some hotels in Britain. Staff attentive, some say too much so. Hot and cold tremors in all rooms. Drugged Premier Cru wine a speciality. Artistic cobweb decorations on walls and furniture a feature.

Countryside: Rather curious with twisted tree trunks and tentacle-like branches. Most trees appear to have been blasted by lightning, brushed aside by monsters or affected by Dutch elm disease. Lay-bys and picnic areas scarce.

Mad scientist: Never gives up trying to make a monster that will look like Charles Boyer, talk like John Gielgud and behave like Shirley Temple. Someone always drops the brain in mud or cinders. Never mind, there's always tomorrow and the next repeat of a repeat.

23

Through a glass wistfully

EDINBURGH detectives, according to a newspaper report, are looking for a thief who smashed a plate glass window and walked away with a fashion dummy at the weekend. The model was abducted from a store in Lothian Road late on Saturday and carried off into the night. When last seen she was wearing a yellow skirt and jacket, a white blouse and an expression of cold hauteur.

The report strikes a deep mellow chord in me as if sounded by a cello playing some adagio as a lament for one's lost youth. Although I deplore the theft as well as the damage to property it may be that I can, as through a glass dimly, understand the feelings of that Lothian Road Lochinvar's actions if they were prompted not by mere avarice or hooliganism but by sentiments stronger than those of ordinary affection.

It is possible that some simple, romantic but misguided lad inclined to let his heart rule his head had fallen under the hypnotic spell of that dummy's elegant sneer and found himself impelled to carry out the action he did to the alarm of the lieges, the annoyance of the shop manager and the irritation of the local gendarmerie who have more pressing matters to investigate in this city of brisk and breezy crime.

There are many males, more than relevant statistics—if any—might indicate, who have been stopped in their tracks when not thinking much about anything by the sight of some model in a shop window striking a poise of coy feminity or strident sensuality and have thought: "Gosh, that's the kind of female I like, trim, neat, pert-looking, with a saucy but not impudent twinkle in the eyes, good clothes sense, fine bone structure, essentially quiet and not a gadabout."

I knew one fellow who used to spend a lot of his spare time gazing in a shop window in Glasgow's Sauchiehall Street at some waxen simulacrum of a refined city female and wishing he could meet someone like her so that could do the honourable thing and plight what he considered was his troth. He never did, the model has now gone and has been replaced by one representing a scowling, "get-on-or-get-out" young male executive about town who wears a suit that looks as if it had been run up by Neanderthal workers in about three minutes with flint tools.

I sympathise with the shop window romanticists because I, even I, once fell for a model in a shop window in Edinburgh's Princes Street—nothing but the best for me—back in the fifties when all the world was young and the hairs on my head resembled the density of a tropical rain forest.

I remember how the sight of her hit me with apocalyptic force as I was walking with the intellectual stoop I was practising at the time—I had the stoop all right, it was the intellectual part I was falling short on—that was giving me fibrostic pains in my shoulders and a mild ache in the centre of my forehead.

She was, I can now say as something conjured up by the genie of the lamp to express my wishful thinking—small, slim, dark, bright of eye, trim of ankle and full of lips that were parted to express perpetual surprise. One delicate hand was placed on a waist that was as perfectly-constructed as a Byronic sonnet and the other, extended eloquently from an arm that to me indicated a life well-spent in calm and harmony, was placed as if to receive a formal and respectful kiss from dignitaries of state and even, I suspected, from the few, remaining crowned heads of Europe. She was wearing a neat navy suit at the time and her price, according to a tag on the jacket, was £5 19s 11½d and, guided by the checks and balances of my economic circumstances, I considered that she represented excellent value for money.

I used to see her at odd intervals during my working day—standing vibrant in the sun—and surrounded by clearly inferior models in ill-fitting or unsuitable ensembles, wholesome as the female spirit of good health that I used to see on the labels of jam jars of malt extract, the contents of which were regularly poured into me by vitamin-enriching parents. Sometimes in the deep Edinburgh night I would see her in the window glow where the new spring or autumn fashions were displayed, the creation of some commercial Pygmalion who probably never suspected the magic that lay in his salary-sullied hands.

Sometimes on those clear, still winter evenings when the breath rose in graceful carbon dioxidal swirls from the chilled mouth and all the city seemed to move with the cold grace of the slow movement of some Beethoven piano concerto, I would pass the window and pay my respects to her realising even in those early days that a barrier, unseen perhaps, but tangible, would always come between us.

She was, of course physically and I suspected spiritually above me. I would never have been able to communicate on her level but in such circumstances I expect silent homage would have been the appropriate action expected of me. In

Stuart Macpherson.

any case I was used to phlegmatic silences on the part of girls I used to take out then, the majority having a vocabulary of approximately 64 words, some of which they used to express disapproval of my views of life, a favourite term of admonition being the withering ... "you're daft."

In fact I used to bring current girl friends along to measure them for size, shape and ethereal qualities against my model who would, I often thought, give me a sort of paned look of reproach. They did not alas compare favourably being for the most part built for durability and utility rather than for mere decoration. They were shaped generally like small potatoes with legs, invariably suffered from some mental malaise, as well as colds spots in their season and, if I remember aright, the effects of over-indulgence in carbohydrates and possible rickets.

I must admit to having a shock when one day I passed the window and realised that my waxen lass was bald and was missing—temporarily, I presumed—an arm, her raised price of £10 15s 6d for a badly-hung summer suit hardly compensating for the disfigurement and disarray. Still, I reflected philosophically, that did not matter as long as she had a leg to stand on and since I myself at that time was beginning to show the first signs of tired hair. I thought that our bare friendly scalps could gleam pinkly together over some winter fireside. Ah, the thoughts and follies of youth. Laugh at them now, they meant so much at the time.

I began losing my taste for her when a male model was placed in the window and the fickle hussy appeared to be concentrating her gaze entirely on the lad who looked like a younger version of the Mexican revolutionary Pancho Villa. It was, I remember one vile Edinburgh night of torrential horizontal rain and bitter vertical winds—late June I expect—when I paid my last respects to her. She was wearing a tarty dress marked down from £8 to £5 17s 6d and was still gazing rapturously at the waxen leering male. I raised my hat and disappeared into the dusk as unmysteriously as I had appeared, saddened but not in the least wiser.

24

At the bar of public opinion

AT the High Court of Grammatical Usage, Mr Justice Syntax presiding, an English adverb known as "Hopefully" pleaded not guilty to charges of conspiracy with persons unknown to corrupt the language, commit a nuisance in and breach of the structure of common sentences as well as maliciously to obstruct the path of clear understanding in phrases used by the lieges and too numerous to be listed in full detail, all contrary to the grammatical jurisprudence of this nation and other English-speaking countries.

The accused was represented by Mr A. Berrant (Sloven, Idiom and Slapdash) and the case for the Queen's English was presented by the well-known language jurist, Mr O.V. Parser (Purist, Predicant & Purge).

As usual in such cases the public benches were packed and many eminent words of the realm, rich in meaning from some of the finest and heaviest dictionaries, were seen.

These included some long ones from pages 213 and 464 of the Shorter Oxford English Dictionary as well as an American visiting party from page 18 "A to K" of Webster's Third International edition.

At the bar of public opinion, "Hopefully," a furtive-looking word who had obviously seen better days, stared hopelessly into the literary distance expecting no doubt a long sentence with no time off for good behaviour.

Mr Parser began by pointing out that the accused had been seen loitering with obvious intent in sentences like:

"Hopefully, British Rail will cut their losses by eliminating all passenger and freight services next year, and "The Portuguese Government are confidently expected to ask Dr Caetano, the former Right-wing Prime Minister to return to power, hopefully next spring." Productions three and five— clippings from newspapers with usually well-informed circles—showed squarely the enormity of the crime.

Mr Parser said that the accused's behaviour was undoubtedly influenced by the rank abuse of the word in America which had in the past grievously ill-treated many of the finest imported English. Hopefully, according to strict grammatical law, meant—and he had learned words of the most eminent dictionaries to substantiate this—"In a manner to raise hope." When the accused appeared in Chambers earlier, the meanings "In a hopeful manner," "With a feeling of hope." and "If all goes well" had been read to him but he had made no reply.

Hopefully's new use was, submitted Mr Parser, illiterate, obscure and ugly. In the examples mentioned—and there were many others—the word did not make clear who was doing the hoping. Thus it cloaked the sentence in ambiguity, making it liable to mislead those to whom it was addressed.

For the accused, Mr Berrant pleaded common usage for Hopefully's action. It was in a sense Lex non scripta—the unwritten Law—of the language that made English the dynamic tongue it was today. Other words—Regina v Prestigious was a case in point—had changed their meaning and use and his client had felt entitled to follow their prestigious path. He had meant no harm, was in a sense easily led and in any case did not think his action was particularly meaningful.

Finding accused guilty, Justice Syntax said ignorance was no excuse in grammatical law. Hopefully's behaviour was just another example of eroded standards in speech and writing that were all too common these days, resulting from half-baked educational methods, the pipe dreams of Socialist pundits and teachers too busy living in cloud cuckoo land to give youngsters a firm educational grounding. He would not say more lest he was accused of political bias, but he hoped that those who found themselves tempted to use Hopefully in a wrong manner would take serious note of what he said. The accused was led off for a long corrective sentence in which he will reflect on the error of his ways . . . hopefully.

25

Where egos dare

I N the morning when in my bed I lie in vacant or in
pensive mood, steeling myself to face the brave new
grey commercial dawn, when the wisps of dreams are
still being brushed from the mind and thoughts are only
half-warmed and quarter-formed, a pleasant little ritual
takes place which never fails to brace me for the wreckful
siege of the most battering day.

It is the arrival of my ego with a broad beam of
confidence—possibly misplaced—in its eyes. "What's the
world like out there?" I ask, sometimes more in resignation
than in hope. "It's as cold as the Antarctic, about as friendly
but sort of bracing and if you can just keep your chin in,
lead with your left and keep your footwork nice and neat,
you might just last out the day with a bit of luck."

I look out of the window at the fading neon of the winter
stars, and stare at the bitter icing of frost on the old fruit and
nut cake of the earth. "Look's pretty hostile," I say,
wondering if I should go back to bed for a year in the hope
that things will improve.

"Got to face it, sir," says my ego, handing me some
warm, nourishing self-esteem and pulling me up by my
bootlaces. Looking at my large wardrobe of attitudes I
select a nice deep-set prejudice today, cut on the bias and
with well-formed shoulder chips to provide ratiocinative
bulk. A man, no matter what the circumstances, should
always keep up appearances. A little amour propre," says
my ego, applying the spray of self-indulgent mist about me

117

and arranging neatly my emotional postures in front so that I can make my choice for the day.

"I think I'll be world weary with a faint dash of hopelessness for the decline of the West," I say sombrely but my ego objects. "You were that yesterday, sir, and the day before. If I might lay out a quiet mixture of wary confidence with matching optimism and a touch of determination not to be ignored by the world under any circumstance I think that might suit the young gentleman best." "Oh, all right," I say moodily. "you know best." I never argue with my ego. What's the point; it always wins.

When I was small, my ego was small—shaped rather like a shining hard conker. It went everywhere with me and had some terrible things done to it by rival egos. When I became older it assumed the size and general consistency of a football, a shape—in Scotland at any rate—that I found to my cost was instantly provocative.

Now it has the bulk and characteristics of a very large balloon, possible not as large as that sent up by the brothers Montgolfier but of a presence to make other egos think twice about colliding with it.

Of course everywhere I go my ego comes too. If I attempt to go out alone, its eyes droop and it emits a mournful sound like wind coming out of a tyre. "Oh come on then," I tell it and before you could say: "Great Freudian Scot," it is tugging me out for a walk like an over-eager puppy fleeing from the nearest worming powder.

Certainly it soars whither other egos dare and there is often a near-inextricable tangle as it tries to get them down for two falls and a submission. It likes in particular female egos which are generally smaller, more delicate but can be as tough as a Brazil nut with armour plate.

My ego's approach is endearingly predictable: "I am a male ego," it says winningly. "Boom. Boom. You are a female ego. Peep. Peep." This often causes the female ego to change to a becoming angry pink and burst into flames and I walk off with my ego as unperturbed and stately as some old Zeppelin ambling over Europe.

My ego and I are essentially a team, each supporting the other in mutual congratulatory and sympathetic action. Sometimes I will have a bad day and crawl home rumbling like a wounded bull elephant. Gosh, there's my ego waiting for me with friendly words like: "Yeah, what does he know about it? That was telling him. He needed that. Of course, you're right. You're older than he is and are therefore bound to know better."

In my youth my ego was peculiarly sensitive, always getting punctured, stood on or crushed by the coarseness of this gross world. Occasionally some girl whose poor judgment of my character was reinforced by her unerringly-aimed barbed verbal shafts at the soft belly of my ego would make my friend shrink with a despairing hiss to about the size of half a water wing. Then I would apply the psychological puncture repair and tell it: "She must be out of her tiny mind to refuse to go out with you. YOU, a king among school-boys. A titan. Stern but just."

Soon, oh very soon, my ego would fill up again and once more soar wildly into the sky, bumping joyously against other egos at the end of their tether and almost hauling me up with it.

You are, in fact, never alone with an ego and a good house-trained one, ever ready to be a companion in your hour of need is something that no intelligent human should be without.

I have a close relationship with my ego which has lasted for many valuable years. Nevertheless I sometimes have my moments of insecurity about how it really feels about me and probe its attitudes mercilessly. "Who do you think is the finest, noblest person you have ever encountered?" "You are, sir," it says with hardly a pause for consideration.

Satisfied, I sometimes turn to Miss Angela Primstone, chatelaine of the columar wine cupboard, who has an ego too but keeps it under firm maidenly control. "What do you really think of me, Miss Primstone?" I sometimes ask her because I want to know. "You are without doubt the most perfect gentleman I have ever had the fortune to encounter in a singularly varied life," she will say unhesitatingly.

There you are, world. A man who is loved by his ego and admired by Miss Primstone cannot be all bad.

26

Forward to the Dunkirk spirit

AS soon as I read the details of the Government's latest measures to prevent this reeling realm from collapsing in ruins like their economic policy, tears mingled with what might have been blood, sweat and vintage Chateauneuf du Pape fell from my eyes, already bloodshot from continually reading about Britain's terrible plight.

In less time than it takes to say "U-turn," I went to the place where you complain about governments. The man at the counter greeted me with courteous attention. "You're here again, sir," he said. "It seems no time since you came to hand in your Army General Service Medal in protest about the Labour Government's defence cuts and your General Certificate of Education because you were not included in the honours' list and because of reports of alleged illiteracy and innumeracy among teachers at the chalk face in Britain's schools. What are you handing in this time?"

From the deep, dark depths of my heavy-duty waterproof-shanked 1956 overcoat I produced an object that has for long been a treasured possession in my cabinet of schoolboy memories along with *The Plain Boy's Guide to British Birds, Miracles of Pond Life,* several ruined conkers and a school report card with the glowing, heart-felt behavioural reference: "Albert has been unusually irritating and inattentive this term," and handed it reverently and regretfully to the man who peered at it closely.

"What's this then?" he asked because he wanted to

know. "It's my wolf cub woggle," I explained, "used for holding together the strands of a cub neckerchief, in this case that of the 150th South Edinburgh ('Toddlers from Hell') Pack."

"I am handing it back," I added, "in protest at the way this Government and every government since the war have let this country down by being too vague and wishy-washy in fulfilling their electoral pledges, too doctrinaire, too stupid stern or too foolishly weak."

"Just let me get that down," muttered the man writing furiously . . . " 'too foolishly weak'. Got it."

I leaned across the counter and heedless of whether all or nobody among the many other complainants heard me, went on: "Just let me say this, that when I received this woggle I regarded it as the highest honour that could be paid to a seven-year-old having had to master the mysteries of the running bowline, the intricacies of the sheetbend and the clove hitch as well as two round turns and a half hitch, recite long passages from Kipling's *Jungle Book* and be able to tell at a glance of my infant eyes on which side of a tree—any tree—moss grew so that I could find the direction north."

"I know just how you feel sir," said the man starting a new page. "I was a Boys' Brigade lad myself. That taught me that life was stern and earnest. Today's kids don't know they're born."

"After all, I continued, "I gave long years of selfless and entirely unpaid devotion to the art of taking stones out of horses' hooves and being clean in thought, word and deed. I could personally recite the poem *If* blindfolded and with my hands tied behind my back. I wonder if any of our so-called leaders could do that and equally I wonder how many could find true north from a moss-covered tree. Most of them only seem to know about west because that is the way this country is going."

"You know, sir," said the man gazing at me thoughtfully in between sentences, "if there were more people like you this country would be in a different position from what it is today."

"Let me say this," I added. "I have, in my electoral life, voted for Labour, Conservative and Liberal and sometimes had to be restrained from voting for all three at once, so eager was I that this country should have an effective government at last.

"I have lived through MacMillan's 'Never had it so good' days, Harold Wilson's so-called white-hot revolution, Edward Heath's three-day week, through inflation, stag-flation, deflation and 'stop-go' economic policies, watched industry grind—as it always does in Britain—to a halt and saw the inevitable trade union coach and horses being driven through government wage restraint policies and 'derisory' management offers to men."

"I mean I've seen life; these middle-aged eyes have observed price rises fail to be ended at a stroke, balance of payments fail to be met continually, though electoral pledges assured us that they would meet, even if only at infinity like parallel lines, and I have seen attempted legislation in place of strife end up in even greater industrial chaos than ever.

"It is," I continued, "too much to ask of the average British working man who only wants a quiet life and who has no axe to grind, except his just demands for shorter working hours, larger wage increases and a decent chance to augment his holidays with the occasional bracing strike to stimulate the adrenalin of men and management alike and bring the healthy flush of combat to their cheeks."

"I wish I had shorthand," said the man scribbling furiously, "but I think I've got the gist of what you say. Basically, you're dissatisfied with the state of the country. Would that be it?"

I nodded agreement. "This isn't the first time I've felt like protesting about the way this country is administered by people who have obviously had no experience of being in or running a Wolf Cub pack. Could Sir Geoffrey Howe rub two pieces of wood together and produce a flame to light a campfire? Could Margaret Thatcher tell which direction she was travelling in using only a wrist-watch and the sun?"

The man shook his head. "I don't expect so, sir," he said writing with head bowed in what I thought must be shame at the revelation that hopeless incompetents were leading the wolf pack that was Britain today and that Akela might be the worst of the lot.

"Who," I asked, "will this country turn to in her hour of need? People with no knowledge of *Scouting for Boys*, and *Orienteering for the under-eights* and who would not know the difference between the Boy Scouts and the Wolf Cubs' promise and *Lady Chatterley's Lover* or someone like myself, skilled in recognising spoors ranging from that of the caracal lynx to the wapiti or wildebeeste?"

"It's pretty obvious, sir," said the man resting for a moment to halt the onset of writer's cramp, "and I don't have to say who will be the backbone of the nation when the crunch comes, the red alert shows and the balloon goes up."

"Of course I suspect," I said, "That the real trouble with Britain is that this nation is uncomfortable in prosperity and likes to be fighting economically or militarily against great odds. In fortress Colditz that is Britain today we are once more tightening our belts and have our backs against the wall and soon there is bound to be a call for the Dunkirk spirit and references to 'standing alone' and 'our finest hour.' " "Don't say," I said, about to leave, "that I haven't warned everyone."

"I'll make a point of underlining that," said the man, who added that if necessary I could look in from time to time and see that the woggle was safe. "And if you find anything else to protest about, say VAT, the Common Market and the Minimum Lending Rate, don't hesitate to hand in something else." "Oh, all right then," I said, and melted into the grey Edinburgh background as mysteriously as I had come.

27

Angles away

DO you see those hands? Artistic, sensitive hands, ones that were made for a virtuoso performance on the violin, for evoking the cold, crystalline clarity of notes in the *Moonlight Sonata,* for painting delicate miniatures and possible, though I would dispute this, ritual strangling.

What have they done so far? Cleaned cars, washed dishes, occasionally mopped the floor and polished up the handle of the big front door. They have also been heavily engaged in pounding typewriters and dropping onto paper wriggling shorthand outlines, the hieroglyphic imps that were created by Sir Isaac Pitman, whose system of curves and angles transformed the art of commercial communication.

I see that Sir James Pitman, a grandson of Sir Isaac, died the other day. He was a proponent of the Initial Teaching Alphabet which he designed with a view to simplifying the learning of the English language but although research showed that children did learn faster with ITA, it remained a minority activity for enthusiasts.

I am sorry that Sir James's idea did not have greater success although I was, like many others, never entirely convinced of his claims that children would have no difficulty in transferring from ITA to traditional spelling.

The name of Pitman is, however, one that immediately evokes for me a picture of an ingenious inventor of a shorthand that is with us yet, despite rival systems, new office high-technology and tape-recorders.

In me you see an example of Pitmanic man from whom straight lines and whorls come as easily on the page as lapidary phrases and superbly-sculpted sentences.

The shorthand gospel, according to Sir Isaac, was for me a wild call and a clear call that could not be denied and all I asked was a strong nib and notebook, and a circle "s" and a grammalogue and a neat "shun" hook.

For those who have not followed the true lineal paths and accepted the scriptic wisdom of that system and who know not what certain references in the last paragraph mean, let me say that they are technical props in the system that cunningly elongates or shortens straight lines and curves as if they were made of Plasticine so that they enable writers' hands to fly across the page, taking down the lightest utterance of some speaker, even, if needed, the sound of a nose sniff or throat clearance, and enabling them to be easily transcribed into written or typed longhand.

At one time all aspiring and perspiring journalists had to have a working knowledge of shorthand, most of them being converted instantly to the broad catholic church of the system invented by Sir Isaac.

A few, who clung to esoteric and heretical beliefs, with a zealousness that probably was not worthy of a better cause, were disciples of the Gregg or Dutton systems which to us pure and righteous Pitmanites, looked on the page like the wicked and dangerous scrawl of idolatry.

I remember when I was a tyro Pitman lad with only a few ramshackle outlines—similar in construction to a Bleriot monoplane—to my name, wondering if I would ever soar with propelling pencil and rotary sharpener to the lofty heights of speed-writing.

My teacher, a stern woman in charge of a class that

consisted of about 30 young females of robust Edinburgh outlines learning to be good secretaries and mothers and four uneasy males, learning to mind their manners and know their place in the bracing air of shorthand tuition, would say to me with typical acidulousness: "With characters like that, you will never get off the ground. They look," she said in fancy flight, "like rows of badly-arranged barbed wire stretched across First World War trenches."

If I went aloft, incumbent on the commercial air of Edinburgh with my kind of shorthand equipment, I would not, she claimed, last ten minutes against the deadly Red Barons of the boss class who, with their staccato rat-tat-tat of directives for notebooks, would shoot me down in blushing flames. "With a shorthand speed of eight words a minute and with outlines drawn on the page and shaded, rather than written, I was heading for a very big fall when I came within range of office dictatorial ack-ack.

Well, I persevered, banking on steep angles on the page to pull me through difficulties, slithering round on aerodynamic curves and looping—I remember as if it was the week before last—my first perfect loop.

Once, some "p" and "b" struts came away on the wings of my words and I had, in a sense, to climb out on the shaky fabric of my outlines to replace them, while I sensed that the class screamed silently as I carried out the perilous manoeuvre. There was one occasion—almost too terrible to mention—when one of my curves began to straighten out and I found myself diving steeply through the paginal lines, out of control, "n" hooks straining, and dots and dashes signalling for help, and heading for a sickening crumple of shapes at the corner of the notebook.

With rapidly-acquired skill and—who knew?—a bit of

Pitmanic luck, I pulled out just in time and taxied to the end of the page with only a few sentences missing and a couple of outlines buckled but otherwise none the worse for my escapade. The shorthand teacher who had accompanied me, watching my frantic pencil and fluttering page, had gone pale under her Edinburgh tan and looked as if she had had a series of light and dark strokes. "Class is over for the day," she said, collapsing like a sagging "f" hook at her desk.

Then one morning, when all Edinburgh stood in bold angular outline against the sky that looked like a blank notebook and the wind was filled with office dust and flying eraser flecks, the teacher said through clenched dentures: "You're going solo today Morris."

I gasped, clutched my pencil like a joy-stick, checked the trim of my notebook, the pages of which were turning over nicely, saw that the lead in my novice's 2B fuselage was as sharp as a ruler rap over the knuckles, swallowed hard, switched on the note-taking ignition, moved along the page and in more time than it takes to write this was in genuine shorthand flight.

I consulted my mental speedometer. It was showing 50, 60, nearly 70 words a minute. I was climbing steeply with rising exhilaration. "The report and accounts are now in your hands and can," I saw on the page instrument dials, "be taken as read . . ."

What joy, what bliss, what poetry of aerodynamic writing was in my hands. I put the pencil's nose down for speed. "By the end of the year, our performance in the retail sector was substantially up on the previous year."

Above the cloud base of commercial activity, my teacher droning steadily, I held the pencil in masterly control:

"Stocks, debtors and creditors at 31 March 1942 are little changed from the previous year..."

There I was careering crazily over the heights of "borrowings and working capital," where "management controls" looked like a relief map of the Himalayas and "trading prospects" seemed like a serpentinal river and hardly had I cleared the low ridge of "group turnover" when the test ended and I made a bumpy but accurate landing on the smooth surface of "profitablity before tax."

Great days and there were greater to come when my speed broke the 100 words a minute sound and sweat barrier and achieved no less but certainly no more than 140 words a minute, with mettle fatigue showing in every angle joint and stress-bending curve.

Today I can still achieve that speed, maybe more, but since all my characters often resemble one shaky line, I doubt if I could read one word back. Still, it's the effort that counts.

Thank you Sir Isaac and my salute to all Pitman disciples. Curves at the ready and angles away.

28

The night runners of Newington

THE Edinburgh night was Wagnerian in its roaring intensity of wind, clouds racing like a stampede of amorphous, mystical beasts and cold, blue, scarcely-winking stars. The sudden gust, bursting into a confused, rain-spattered crescendo of portentous sound seemed to suggest snatches of "The Ride of the Valkyries" and the dying notes of "Gotterdammerung" and hint at the breaking of nations, the dying of civilians, the crashing of trees and the collapsing of giant, heavily-eroded spiritual and temporal standards.

It was a sort of saga night, beloved of chill Northern lands, meant specifically for people to be safely indoors listening to their houses, creak, chimney cans rattle, slates fly and the old gnarled television set telling its always fascinating sexual fairy tales or yarns of jolly, stimulating violence. It was also a night for pitying poor sailors at sea or spending their money like drunken regional governments.

Head bowed into the wind, clothes hauled tight about me I was tackling my way in a walk in the darkened streets of Newington—a popular, moral and healthful suburb of Edinburgh—where none was about save shivering, under-privileged gangs of youths seeking whom they might devour, the lone grafitti painter heroically carrying out his thankless task despite untold discomforts and dangers, cats which for some reason eyed me balefully and the occasional, muffled citizen being yanked spasmodically into walking movement by the leads of their eager, panting, nose-twitching dogs.

Suddenly above the war song of the gale, I heard a curious pattering noise, becoming louder, curiously frightening and similar, I imagine, to the sounds which petrified poor old "Wind in the Willows" Mole when lost in the Wild Wood. Then, from behind me, with a collectively-agonised sound as of underwater swimmers breaking surface after a long submersion, came a ragged line of young men running.

Dressed—with no regard to the inclemency of the weather and the existence of many draughts—in shorts and singlets, they gave a brief, tantalising glimpse of goose-pimpled limbs reddened by wind and rain, purposeful faces and breath being ejected in short puffs like Victorian steam engines struggling up a gradient before they passed into the night as mysteriously as they had come.

Then more runners came behind them. This time they seemed to be of the female persuasion—chesting up and bottoming out—looking equally determined and making the pavement reverberate with the thunder of their passing. Later two athletically-clad middle-aged men, moving wearily, brought up the rear, making odd little wheezing noises as they passed. "They went that way." I said to them, pointing into the murk of the night. They did not deign to acknowledge my directions but puffed off into the darkness. Later more runners passed me in the opposite directions and for a time it seemed that all Edinburgh South was on the move, like one of the mass European race migrations.

Where are they going, these—for the most part—clean-limbed runners, and from whence have they come? Are they rushing to some far-off Dionysiac revel in, say, the yard of a disused advanced factory, where under a gibbous moon they will leap into wild, uncouth dances, feed on honeydew and drink the cool, nourishing low-caloried milk of paradise? Are they pursued perhaps by terrible and—to us—unseen spirits who will hound them to run forever, like figures on a Grecian urn come to life? Are they indeed human, these swiftly-moving minions of the night? Yes, they are, because when one jostled me accidentally he felt hot, damp but essentially solid.

Perhaps if I see them again I will gird up courage and loins and venture to get to that Nirvana of the night. It is likely however that I will run only about 100 yards before everything goes purple before my eyes. I must really get some more exercise these days.

29

Whiff of blanco

ALTHOUGH my dreams are essentially peaceful there are times when my subconscious mind, accompanied by eye movements that are as rapid as the mechanisms of a Gatling gun, take me back to my military days, about which I am normally reluctant to write, when I bore a musket (all right, it was a short magazine Lee Enfield rifle) in the service of His Majesty King George VI at a time when this country's foes were being hit for six, given a bloody nose and shown the door by the victorious Allies in Europe and the Far East.

Once more I am young Private A. ("take that smile off your face") Morris, helping to make up khaki-clad bulk in the ranks and files at some gaunt, grey, barracks.

It is a cold, wet March morning. A sharp north-easter is sweeping across the barracks' square and the drill sergeant's tongue is lashing out like a cat o' ten tails to say that from what he has seen of us and our military capacity, Britain is not just scraping the barrel but is tearing up the barrel itself.

Then the sergeant is beside me in a flash and himself in a rage. "What did you just do Private Morris?" he asks in a brisk, interested manner, "Wiped my nose sergeant," is the honest and frank answer.

"On the parade ground, you wiped your nose!" he bellows in the dragon's teeth of the military wind. The rest of the ranks and files, noses unwiped, gaze stonily into whitewashed distance. A seagull screams in derisive

134

comment; somewhere in the armed background a piper makes a sound like a warthog dying in a mud pool and in the cold, crisp air, the menacing scent of dinner, like a stone age drainage system, hits the nostrils of the aghast ranks.

"You don't take time to wipe your nose on the parade ground as you don't do it in the field of battle. Do you realise that if we had taken time off to wipe our noses in 1940 Hitler and his hordes might have been across the channel in a jiffy and overwhelmed us before we'd got our handkerchiefs back up our sleeves?"

I nod contritely. There is a noise like a six inch gun firing. "You don't take time to move your head laddie. Off you go and run round the square 26 times and don't use your handkerchief to mop your brow."

I will then wake up in a hot sweat and realise that I had relived a true military incident that took place in my army training days in the Gordon Barracks, Aberdeen, when I was but a simple soldier, eating my food out of highly-polished mess tins, spending much of my days prodding helpless sandbags with rifle-fitted bayonets, attending lectures about personal hygiene in insanitary places in the British Empire and keeping my handkerchief firmly out of sight when any NCO or officer was around.

I am therefore an old Brig of Don man, button-bright, booted, badged and battle-dressed in my platooned day and often clad in field service marching order which topped by a steel helmet two sizes too large for me, made me resemble a small, armed, mobile toadstool.

I learned much at the Gordon Barracks; that if we had any military use at all it was to make Germans and Japanese die laughing that we may have broken our probation officers' hearts but that we would not break those of our drill sergeants and that if we were caught off duty, lounging in the well-kept streets of Aberdeen with a packet of wine gums in one hand and a fish supper in the other, objects that symbolised military slackness, it would go hard with us.

When you look at me you see a bit of military history writ small, a man stiffened by Army porridge, steeled by the heavy-duty, double-repeating barrack sausage and shocked into discipline by the NAAFI bun. After six weeks at the old Gordon Barracks, I was ready to pass out on parade marching but preferably in a stretcher.

I owe the barracks a lot, especially the knowledge that while I would never be a good shot I could change step on the march with the best of the Grenadier Guards and that if Britain ever had her back to the wall again I would be ready to left and right wheel and move into column of threes in a way that would daunt the sternest enemy.

I also learned at my sergeant's elbow and under my regimental sergeant major's chin, my very first Army songs which, after a childhood of singing nothing stronger than "Drink to me only with thine eyes," and "On the good ship Lollipop" came very strangely to sensitive Edinburgh, Newington ears.

They were honest military folk ditties dwelling on the generous physical proportions of certain female minions of the moon, the alleged moral laxity of some ATS NCOs and the myriad faults of the Army, the latter containing a colour and crispness of expression that did one's heart good to hear. When marching en route through the streets of Aberdeen, blue sparks flying from under our boots as nails crashed against granite setts, and looking like massed, lumpen military Mercuries, our ranks were restrained from

Stuart Macgregor.

singing songs that would bring a blush to the cheeks of Aberdeen citizens who were, and I believe still are, a generous, warm-hearted lot, inclined to take the disadvantaged to their bosoms, especially in war-time

At the end of the training when I and the rest of our company were deemed fit to show a healthy brisket to the foe, I left the Gordon Barracks with the feeling of one who has done penance in purgatory under the strict eyes and sharp tongues of NCOs, many of whom had a fine line in biting sarcasm and bayonet-sharp, military humour that would have had us doubling over with laughter in the ranks but for the fact that soldiers did not take time off to do such things.

As one who went through the highly-efficient sausage machine at the Brig of Don where the raw, amorphous mass of civilians were turned into rows of khaki-clad ranks, I still get a sentimental whiff of blanco in my mind's nose when I think about the place. I therefore deplore the news that the training of junior infantry soldiers for Scottish regiments will take place outside Scotland after the closure of the barracks towards the end of next year.

The other day, the Army confirmed the closure of the barracks, at least in its present form, and that its main role will be transferred to Ouston near Newcastle. Junior soldiers will receive six months' initial training there, after which they will go to Glencorse Barracks for adult training.

As an old perspirer, I find it sad that young Scottish soldiers will not tread the ground on which I and countless others had to march and counter-march, present arms and, for that matter, port them for inspection.

Newcastle, excellent city though it is, is no substitute for a place with the character of Aberdeen that gave recruits the feeling that they were not just part of the Army but had a welcome place in a Scottish community.

When I was in hospital blues, the citizens treated me like a returning war hero, men raising their hats in respect and women sometimes plying their handkerchieves over one so young and so brave. I was only recovering from grumbling tonsillitis but no-one would let me pay my fares on buses, for newspapers, meals in restaurants and seats in the cinema; I'll never forget those bountiful northern days.

I urge the military to re-think their plans for the barracks' closure, they have played too big a part in the life of the area to be thus crassly removed. I hope that they will be kept in full working order; after all, why should those who have been through the military mill be the only ones to have suffered?

30

Off the mark

AS many people will know, and as many will have guessed, this column is an ever-open haven for all sorts of syntactic refugees which includes puns strained to screaming point, tortured sentences, unattached and uncared-for participles and brutally-split infinitives.

At the main frontier post there is a plaque which says: "Give me your tired ideas, your poor, outworn adjectives, your huddled adverbial clauses yearning for space, the wretched literary refuse of your teeming wastepaper baskets. Send these sentences, parsing all belief in their length, and your tempest-tossed hyperactive verbs to me. I will indent ten welcoming spaces from my editorial margins and slot them in somehow."

Sometimes, I will stand at the main etymological examination centre and look at a sample of the latest flow of immigrants to arrive on the columnar shores. Many of the would-be members of my word population are in a very poor state, ill-spelled, some appearing in tattered clause and suffering, from a quick medicosemantic glance at their appearance, from paronomasia of the zeugma or protatsis of the onomatopoeia. Prolepsis and litotes are endemic in many of the newcomers, who have obviously suffered much oppressive use in previous sentences, a touch of diaeresis can also be found and incipient metathesis, sometimes requiring a small caesural operation, can be a problem.

The prognosis, however, is excellent and when the newcomers are less than a month in the rich, fertile, columnar lands, breathing its inspirational air and basking in its self-congratulatory sunshine, there is often a marked change for the better among many of them, some verbs, for instance, inactive on arrival to the point of moribundity, showing a rare burst of gratifying life when invited to participate in some mind-nourishing sentence.

Some phrases have grown almost by three metrical feet after being in the column but a short time and there is nothing I like better than being greeted by, say, a small participial adjective glowing with good descriptive health and gratitude at its good fortune in being used by me.

Not every word or phrase is allowed to enter this space. Solecisms, though they can slip in, are generally given what is known in the columnar trade as short shrift. Outworn cliches which can arrive as thick and fast as hot cakes are avoided like the plague. Misrelated participles have also been seen occasionally as well as some examples of false analogy but for the most part, the inspection net is drawn tightly by grammarian border officials to ensure that this space is kept free from literary pollution.

A disturbing new phenomenon in the refugee situation is the large numbers of apostrophes that are turning up and which have been expelled, many before they have had time to collect their own personal possessives, from sentences and signs.

Only the other day I was called to a frontier post to see the latest batch of them waiting, with the timeless patience of the dispossessed, to be allowed through to the lush singularities and pluralities of the columnar lands.

Interviewed, they told a dismal tale of being brusquely ordered to move from long established sentences, where many of them had established deep, meaningful, roots, of being picked out like pips in a pomegranate from words and ordered never to return. Some believed there was an unwritten law among English-writing nations to ban the apostrophe for ever and their pinched little faces worked as I told them that in this column we could always use willing, hard-working blobs to denote the possessive singular and plural and would they please stop snivelling and fall into line.

According to a newspaper report the other day, the apostrophe is being wiped out of written English because it "detracts from the clean lines of a signwriter's type style."

The report quotes a survey in the latest issue of the magazine *Language Monthly* that names the culprits as the large banks, shop signwriters and advertisers.

The catastrophe has also spread to literary associations which now call themselves the Publishers Association and the Translaters Association. It also affects many of the bookshops in Britain.

The magazine criticised cinemas advertising Richard Attenboroughs *Ghandi* although it doubted whether most filmgoers noticed such barbaric efforts. It also cited horrific examples like Todays Tesco, Barclays Bank and Chelsea Mans Shop.

I personally met a refugee from Barnetts Mans Shop which revealed that it had been a well-known grammatical feature of that sign for many years, performing its work conscientiously and even being given a hint of pluralistic promotion, when it was believed that there would be a sign stating Barnett's Men's Shop. It was not, the apostrophe told me bitterly, to be.

Without warning it was given the swift metaphorical boot

and its position was no different from that of thousands of other apostrophes, one of which revealed brokenly that it had been uprooted from a long sentence and told jocularly that it was getting time off for good behaviour.

Some apostrophes, wandering aimlessly in the thin literary air, had taken demeaning jobs in inferior sentences and signs but what else could they do to make a mark in literary life? It was a sad genitival case in which to find themselves.

Some had found work in seedy signs like fish 'n' chips, wash 'n' wipe, beer 'n' byte, gobble 'n' gulp and pick y' own strawberries. At any given time there were masses of unemployed apostrophies, carrying their battered little possessive cases, waiting with diminishing hope of employment in this increasingly illiterate world.

Youths, I understand, are coming on employment stream with little or no knowledge about the correct use of the apostrophe and, I am told by my education spies, that is hardly strange since some teachers show a distinct and disturbing ignorance of its use.

I let all the apostrophes in. Well, I could hardly keep them waiting outside while the winds of English abusage were blowing so keenly about their pinched little bodies. In just the same way I once allowed hopefully to enter, provided it confined its activities to being an adverb and not appear, as in the colloquial meaning—"if all goes well," and prestigeful to denote "full of prestige" thus keeping out what I believe to be the false prestigious, which is now used for that meaning.

Ah, what jubilation there was. The apostrophes made a noise like a row of dominoes toppling into each other, and a refugee from a brutally-oppressive sign. Tea 'n' Toast that hung in a typical Dorset village, next to one marked Egg 'n' Crumpets, moved to a vote of thanks to the generosity of the young columnar squire—"may his possessions and his tribe increase"—the friend of the apostrophe who would always make his columnar mark with one.

"We are in Albert Morris's column, the dot's on the 'i,' the semi-colon's in place, the infinitive's unsplit; all's right with the column's words." A lump came into my throat, a small tear formed in one eye. Did it look like an apostrophe? If it did, it was appropriate.

31

Streetcars of desire

IT is all very well for yesterday's second leader in the paper to draw merriment from the curious story in the *Observer* which told of Mr David Steel narrowly escaping having his head cut off by an overhead tramwire at a place called Galashiel, but for a moment, as fleeting as a snowflake in sunshine or a wisp of memory drifting across the mind, I believed it.

Somewhere in the Liberal leader's constituency—an area of stirring legend, romance, history and often uncomfortable twilight tales of little people—could, I thought, exist a mythical place, in some ways resembling the illustrious Border settlement that has a final "s" to its name, but which is only seldom glimpsed and heard, like the fabled land of Lyonnesse that can, it is said, be seen sometimes in the light of setting western English Channel suns, its turrets and towers spiking the heraldic blazon of the horizon and from which can be heard the tinkle of church bells of the decibel-rating of the horns of elfland faintly blowing.

That, for a wistful second or two, seemed the *Observer's* Galashiel—a shimmering mirage town, perhaps glimpsed in the distant summer haze by the few, where its fabled streets bathed in a rosy glow and flecked with embattled discos, legendary Chinese carry-out shops and the Ali Baba caves of supermarkets, echoed and re-echoed not just to the the hum of the populace but to the evocative clank, screech and grind of the tramcar, an urban mobile construction that many people, including myself, believed almost extinct as

145

the diplodocus and the dodo, the bustle and the beehive hairstyle for women.

In real-life Galashiels, where no tramcar heaves its metal bulk along its throbbing thoroughfares and the night sky is not lit by star clusters of sparks from metallic rods on tram roofs touching overhead wires, people would talk in a mixture of wary speculation and downright unease about the place that uncannily had a similar name to their own town.

To see Galashiel, in all its shining, enticing, faery forms with shop notices displaying cut-price washing-up liquid, closing-down sales in various emporia and the fabulous *Return of Dracula's Daughter* showing at the local cinema was bad enough and could presage some doom-laden event such as an imminent visit to the optician but to enter it, was, apart from the ever-present danger of having one's head instantly removed from one's body by overhead tram-wires, something that should be avoided at all reasonable cost.

There, the entranced visitor, suddenly stumbling into the town, could be lulled by the siren-song of the tramcars, vehicles built like the control towers of 1916 dreadnought battleships, driven by gnarled and forbidding uniformed gnomes and conducted by alluring creatures resembling women who would warble in their native woodnotes wild: "Two more upstairs, the rest inside."

Enter them and you could be lost for a long time like Thomas the Rhymer in fairyland and emerge after what seemed a century later, babbling o' strange journeys to enchanted termini where darkness spreads her jealous wings and the night jukebox sings, where conductresses sing Martha, oh Martha, the rambling witch of the wood..." as with centuries-old cunning, they punch tickets to eternity and passengers sit pale and wondering like the night at arms in certain lines by the poet Keats.

On the other hand I can see the trams in the *Observer's* dream-like Galashiel as vehicles, mainly of the mind, that could transport one back in time, say to a favourite period of life, like late childhood or early manhood. "A 2d one to 1936," I see myself telling the conductor, an elfin creature with a merry smile and a laugh like a banshee when she informs people waiting to be transported to the past: "Sorry, full up . . ."

She may accept my fare and tell me exactly what minute of my life to get out at or she may shake her head and say: "Sorry, we go no further than 1943. Get off at 1951, take the 1926 red-coloured tram headed 'General Strike' and ask to be let off at 1937. You can walk from there, it'll only take you eight months, four if you run."

I see myself sitting on the top deck watching the fragmented years flash back with people in the garb of 1963 standing at authorised stops, others whistling hit tunes of 1959 crossing forgotten roadways and perhaps some creature in Teddy Boy garb creeping on crepe soles in the time-rich shadows.

Eventually, I will get to my destination where the air will be filled with the sound of Henry Hall and his dance band playing: "The music goes round and round," the bustle of the streets, the noise of the horseless carriages and of course the ever-present cold, metallic, rumble of the great tramcars gliding endlessly on through time and pre-determinate motion.

In my mind, the tramcars of the past still sail like great steel argosies in city streets in movements as smooth as a skater on ice, which coarse, quivering and jolting buses could never hope to achieve.

I can see them, the superb trams of Edinburgh moving primly and purposefully along the streets of my past, the far-venturing No 14 that took one of the docklands of Leith where jaunty mariners, their eyes containing far-away looks as if constantly seeking distant havens in which they could refresh themselves, would board and occasionally sing to themselves or to the passengers at large, songs of speculation about insobriety among sailors, the No 3 that would convey one with safe passage to the far-off, semi-rustic haunts of Stenhouse or the superbly-upholstered No 6 that forever, like an artificial satellite rounding the globe, circled Marchmont and beyond conveying passengers of refinement and high moral tone.

Ah, my tramcars of desire; I used to dream about them years after they had ground to oblivion and museums, and the dreams always brought a sudden rush of happiness on seeing the grand old vehicles rumble up out of the purple Edinburgh dusk, lights ablaze and stern but just drivers at the helm. It was like a return to the days of my youth, to the lightness of boyhood, to a world of strange transportive joy that perhaps can exist only in dreams and which fades with the dawn wind and the light dying in morning stars.

I envy Mr Steel in being permitted by fate and journalism to enter tram-haunted Galashiel and express my thankfulness that he did not lose his shrewd and finely-chiselled head as a result of the experience.

I must also send my sympathy to him in his virus affliction, my hope of his speedy recovery and tell him that if ever he runs on a "bring back the tram" ticket, he will have this column's full and unswerving support to the terminus and beyond.

32

To the Ogaden and back

WHEN people look at me—as they often do and who can blame them?—they see not only Morris the man, the journalist and legend in his lifetime but a piece of British Imperial history writ small.

As is well known I do not like to talk of my experiences under palm and pine, of keeping the sun from setting on what was the British Empire, dealing with lesser breeds without the law and of the days when I shot straight (well, reasonably straight), kept clean, feared the glass-house and honoured the Queen, although it was the King in those distant days as I expect some of you will remember.

Now that I am on the subject, however, I might as well reveal without breaching the Official Secrets' Act that I, even I, have been in the Ogaden, that area of sun and sand, fleas and flies, desert, dust and dancing mirages which is now the subject of violent dispute between the Somalis and Ethiopians and which when I had the honour of helping to maintain a British Sanders-of-the-River-type presence there, was a land of singular quietness, order, respect for authority and comparative prosperity.

I do not say that I was in any way responsible for that felicitous state as I was then but an Army corporal and small for my age and with only a Deanna Durbin picture in my knapsack; I merely mention the facts as I knew them.

What I want to make clear is that I know the terrain and while memory has naturally dimmed the outline of each and every boulder, I still remember with sunbright clarity the long, brown serpentine churnings of the rivers Webi Shebeli and the Juba. The latter I often crossed by rope and raft ferry while singing natives hauled the craft with commendable good humour and crocodiles gazed with biding-their-time look in their eyes at the pink-and-white, soft-centred British soldiery that lazed nonchalantly on the craft's bulwarks.

I was stationed for a short time at a settlement called Daghabur at which each day we paraded under a somewhat frayed Union Jack, stamped our highly-polished boots in the parade ground, got our native troops to ground and present arms, change steps on the march and salute with a snap and punctilio that must have shortened the lives of agitated desert flies that hovered in the clouds of blanco dust continually rising from the sweating ranks.

All the techniques of modern warfare that could be taught were shown to the Somali troops by the ever-generous British Army—porting arms for inspection, darning socks at the halt, saluting on the march, burnishing mess tins until they could have been used to send heliograph messages across the lone and level sands, and laying out equipment for kit inspection with architectural neatness and precision.

Your average Somali chap picked up all these things—and many more when we weren't looking—with alacrity. Many of our NCOs and officers felt that they were with us up to the hilt although when the hilt was reached there might be a tendency for them to go their own way.

An acknowledgement of the fact that they had gone their own way before could be seen in a memorial in the small harbour of Berbera to the British and colonial troops who had fallen in the campaigns against Mohammed Abdalla

Hasan "the Mad Mullah," who from 1900 until 1920 had fought against British authority.

I expect a statue to him has replaced the memorial at the port which is now said to be a Russian naval base and which once knew the steady reassuring tramp of my boots, signifying each hot, salt-windy day to the wondering natives, Pax Britannica and the ceremonial opening or closing of the quartermaster's stores of which I had the honour to be in charge.

From time to time my military duties took me all over the area where I gazed patronisingly at villages and nodded reassuringly at their residents. The last war was well over by that time but I felt it my duty to keep going through some of the motions. Occasionally I would raise myself through the hatchway in the roof of my Army truck cabin and sweep the horizon through field glasses. It was an impressive action that I think helped to keep the Somalis in awe.

Of course I was often sent to Dere Dawa, one of the towns now at the centre of the fighting. As a British Army corporal with quite large stripes on his sleeves I was obviously an object of much respect among the natives who had an eye for natural leaders with good military bearing.

Addis Ababa, the capital, was within easy camel lope and I was given one or two hints that the then Emperor Haile Selassie of whom some of you may have heard, might send for me to ask for advice, military or civil, on how to run his vast and ancient country. The fact that he never did caused me no perturbation. I merely put it down to bad counselling or deliberate obstruction from government or court officials jealous of their reputations. Had he done so, conditions might have been very different in that far-flung part of the world today.

I would like to think that in the present hostilities there are some fellows in the Somali ranks who, if not actually trained by me, were instructed by those to whom I had the privilege and pleasure of telling all I knew about the grand old Clausewitzean craft of soldiering.

Are there even now, I wonder, some chaps going into action with brass belt buckles so brightly brassoed that the gleam would nearly blind an enemy unexpectedly exposed to them? Are there those who can change step on the march with a rhythmic shuffle that would do credit to Fred Astaire and those who can affright the very air by porting arms for inspection and easing the springs of their rifles in a way that is charged with incipient menace?

I have seen some recent pictures of Somali warriors going into action and frankly I am just a little disappointed at their turn-out. We would not have had these chaps in my outfit. I cannot see them forming threes in the face of the enemy with any real effectiveness and I suspect, although I have no proof, that they do not polish their mess tins.

I do not believe that I have been forgotten in the towns, villages, water-holes and baracks of Somalia where I expect they speak of "Corporal Four-eyes Morris" yet. Because of this I expect any day now a phone call to ask if I would like to give the chaps a help-out with my expertise and knowledge of the lay of the land.

"Any phone message from Somalia or runners with cleft-sticks?" I asked Miss Angela Primstone, chatelaine of the columnar wine cupboard this morning. "None so far, Mr Morris," she replied with customary if dismaying accuracy. Oh well, since the Ogaden obviously needs me I expect the call will come eventually. Don't you?

33

Marching on a full stomach

ALTHOUGH I had a distinguished military career earning the coveted description "honest sober and trustworthy" on my demobilisation papers I am essentially a man of peace and therefore reluctant, unless pressed or if the mood is on me, to talk about my Army experiences and my contribution—unavailing alas—towards keeping the sun from setting on the Empire.

To look at me now striding with erect soldierly bearing among the slouchers in our city streets who would not know a Bakelite button stick from Army Form 215 (c) Requisition for Officer's Trouser Presser, you would hardly believe that I survived all the rigours of Army life including daily advances on cookhouses where braving all in the course of dutiful and patriotic eating, I tackled with fork jab and bright blade countless helpings of what was then known tersely but colourfully as "grub."

Apart from an occasional twitch of painful reminiscence across my finely-honed features and the curious shadows that play about my eyes as if they had seen things on a plate too terrible to mention in civilised society I emerged practically unscathed from the Army's gastronomic front-line.

As a veteran military eater I was therefore surprised and just a bit indignant at the report that appeared in this paper yesterday which stated that troops at Strensall Barracks, near York, were so well fed that up to 150 meals a day were thrown away to feed pigs.

John Becket (58), a kitchen hand, of Haxby, near York, admitted the theft of two unfired, heavy-calibre rump steaks at the barracks. He was caught during a routine check as he left the camp with the steaks on the front seat of his car. In court it was said that on one occasion 155 complete meals were thrown away and one morning after breakfast 100 fried eggs went into the swill bin.

What, I ask, is going on in Britain's fattened forces? More to the point—do the military authorities realise that by stuffing troops with all these proteins and carbohydrates they are breaking a time-honoured tradition, hallowed since the days of the battle of Minden and before, that Britain's fighting services should exist only on the minimum amounts of nourishment and that should be so badly cooked that the men will become incensed and eventually work out their rage and hunger on the enemy, puffling and waddling adiposally into battle.

I can see the situation in some future conflict. The scene will be the front line near the small German industrial town of Bad Oder and the 1st Battalion the Queen's Own Comestibles will be manning a defensive position, rifles Krupp-manufactured eating irons, heavy-duty napkins, campaign-quality cartridge belts of pepper and salt paper tubes and field service packets of tartar sauce (sharp as a bayonet thrust) at the ready.

A sergeant battle-wise in the ways of Army eating will run his eye, stern but with a brightly-burnished twinkle, over the lads, some not more than 19 but all weighing over 16 stones although the majority are still only shaving their double or triple chins twice a week.

"Keep your eyes to your front," the sergeant will snarl, "you're not in the Ritz buttery now swigging down the claret with the Veal Holstein. Here you're going to have to rough it with onion soup, mussels in white wine, lamb Beatrice, medallions de boeuf duchess and before the Ruskies come at us, maybe a nice bit of field service blackcurrant sorbet, a slice of regimental chocolate cake all washed down with individual canteens of Chateau Leoville Poyferre '64."

"Stop moaning Private Pritchard 364, you may have broken your mess waiter's heart but you're not going to break mine."

Suddenly the terrible sounds of war will break out: from the east will come a noise like that of a distant but advancing forest fire. It will be that of massed Russian divisions eating crusty black bread and drinking soup made with stock from boiled down World War surplus boots and taking enormous slugs of military vodka that tastes like hornet's blood.

Then will come the slow, menacing, sound of massed indigestion as the robot men from the east unmask their crude but effective anti-acid tablets. The men of the 1st Comestibles, pausing only in mid-chew to take from the last offer of the cheese board, short, squat, ugly but effective slices of double repeater stomach-riddling .300 Parmesan mined from the interior of a lofty EEC cheese mountain, will adjust smartly their battlepack polyunsaturated fat margarine pouches, hold their fire until they see the Asiatic crumbs on the enemy's lips and then all culinary hell will no doubt be let loose.

I just hope our rump fed lads will be able to hold their own side of the table against the Ruskies who despite Salt are not military eating experts tell me, above treacherously drinking red wine with the fish and vice versa with all that that entails, etc.

I myself believe in a bracing austerity in Army cookhouses that will bring the harsh realities of military life to new recruits and show them that they are not wearing the Queen's uniform for pleasure alone.

In my Army days, a cookhouse could almost have been an extension of an assault course and maybe the frontline itself. They used to be mephitic places of Gothic gloom shrouded in steam and smoke through which pallid warriors would peer and grope to line up for what passed as food and then to find stark wooden benches by stark wooden tables there to view the stark contents on their plates.

In some corner soldiers on perpetual fatigue duty laboured like lost souls in Dante's inferno to wash up huge mounds of used plates and then pile them in rows of Pisa-tower-leaning columns around them.

Sometimes the hubbub of troops talking and attempting to eat would be shattered momentarily as a column of plates tilted like some forest giant and crashed heavily on to the sawdust of the floor, giving the lads a passable imitation of a howitzer shell exploding nearby and sending ATS cooks and officers running to the scene of destruction, chattering with rage and shrilling their contempt for men and their ways and works.

In my training days we had to eat our food in superbly polished mess tins, getting the soup in one tin and the main course, sweet and—if we insisted—the tea all at once in the other. This system introduced us to new and sometimes exciting tastes and one day, following a famous literary precedent, I arose, made my way to an ATS corporal with a face like a fireman's axe and asked for another helping of brussels sprouts apparently crushed for our consumption by rifle butts.

"Wotyerfinkthisisbleedin Savoy?" the military maiden asked in tinkling tones. I made a strategic withdrawal under the fire of her eyes and never asked again. You learned about life in the old cookhouses. Get some service in and get your stew browned, laddies; you don't know the half of it yet.

34

My slow, quick memory

AS an ex-Newingtonian, still somewhat ill-at-ease in the alien corn of Morningside, I was standing at my new bus-stop yesterday, idly speculating on the inscrutable workings of fate, the passage of time and the laggard passing of our municipal argosies, when my eye caught sight of a building, now derelict and which, I learned later, was to be occupied by a supermarket.

The buidling, forlorn and decrepit was, I realised with the shock of a cold douche of reality on warm memory, the old Plaza where I received my baptism of dancing fire and in the fabric of which must be the ghosts of thousands of young hopefuls seeking future husbands or wives or merely someone who could get round in a double-spin chasse reverse turn without crashing into the wall, other couples or crushing their partner's feet while trying to execute a step, known technically in dancing school circles, as "the twinkle."

Now, alas, I suppose the building awaits its last ball—the demolition one. I, and no doubt thousands of others who quick-quick-slowed and eyed the line-up of the opposite sex with shrewd fancier's appraisals or nervous and embarrassed eyes, will mourn therefore.

It was here, even here, where I, and other lads who had been through the rigours of the dancing schools, died the deaths of a thousand cuts from prospective partners. In the dance-schools, the walls of which were lined with mirrors in which we could see ourselves gazing pallidly over the shoulders of our stoic instructresses, we solemnly went through the regulation waltz, the statutory quick-step and the obligatory fox-trot until we were adjudged fit to try out our rythmic limbs on the unsuspecting girls who, aflame with the glow of lipstick and rouge, were to be seen en masse around the dance-hall floor gazing determinedly into the middle distance, sneering elegantly at their nails or chewing, with the rotary action of the larger ruminants, endless supplies of gum.

The dance halls of Edinburgh were, in my youthful dancing days, sharply different in character and clientele. The Plaza tended—although there were some marked exceptions—to get a type of dancer who could parse a sentence and who could tell with hardly a moment's hesitation, between the weave and the fish-tail steps that the square on the hypotenuse of a right-angled triangle equalled the sum of the squares on the other two sides.

In the Plaza, where there always seemed to be a plethora of medical students and embryonic executives, you could have what passed for intelligent conversations with your partner as she averted her face aloofly from your gaze as if you were something a pure food committee had rejected. When you were refused a dance, it was often done with a perfect grace that merely gave your ego a sort of dull thud, rather similar I imagine to what an assegai must feel like between the shoulder blades.

"No thanks, I'm resting," some fair damsel, who looked like the descriptions of a wispy maiden out of Tennyson's "Idylls of the King," would say. You would then gulp and die a little but with the resilience of youth recover sufficiently to receive another cut from some other female three minutes later. A lot of females seemed to be resting,

you began to notice after a while. Rush up to them with the eagerness of a puppy after a bone and suddenly they would seem to sag against the wall and adopt an attitude of terrible weariness. It was as baffling as it was disappointing but you learned to live with it.

In the Palais. Fountainbridge, conversations tended to be monosyllabic and three and a half grunts were adjudged to be a long and complicated discourse. There, the females were lined up like yearlings at Tattersalls and their fetlocks and flanks studied and general mobility adjudged for trial gallops in "She Wore Red Feathers and a Hula-Hula Skirt," or a brisk canter to the mellifluous, melting strains of "The Blue Tango."

There, refusals to dance were crisp and to the point, resembling a sudden stab with a stiletto. I remember one night going there with a friend who resembled a sort of Edinburgh cut-price, cut-down version of the late Errol Flynn. His hair was beautifully creamed and slicked back until it resembled the cold glow of marble, his shirt of snow-blinding whiteness and his regimental tie, the Brigade of Guards—he had actually served with the Army Catering Corps—matched superbly his immaculate blazer with anchors on the buttons. Those, with knife-like creases on his discreetly-grey flannels, expensive shoes and his boyish, roguish smile and gleaming teeth had made him irresistible in, he claimed, a thousand dance halls in Britain.

Alas, he had not reckoned on the cruel fact that such a garb was anathema to the clientele of the Palais, who, if male, tended to wear long jackets that reached nearly to their knees with padded shoulders that made their backs resemble the rear of warehouses. They also flaunted drain-pipe trousers and crepe-soled shoes that made the wearer feel and sometimes behave as if he were dancing on a trampoline.

My friend rushed up to a female, large of eyelash, dramatic of mascara and flaxen of hair and with stiletto heels that made her young body sag forward to resemble a famous leaning tower. "I wonder," he began in his courtly way and flashing his teeth, eyes and buttons, "if you would care to have this dance with me?" The girl looked at him with terrible silent scorn, pondering on the unusual length of his request while shifting her chewing gum from one cheek to the other. She then answered with lethal Edinburgh and Lothian directness. "Nu't," she said and pivoted smartly on one heel and clicked off to be joined by a male partner the backs of whose hands seemed to brush long the floor as he walked.

My friend seemed to shrink, the twinkle went out of his eyes, the lustre from his Pepsodent-smile teeth and even the gleam of his buttons suddenly seemed tarnished. He had been rejected; it was the Palais equivalent of the black ball for membership at Whites.

Ah, dear old dancing days. What heartaches, what thrills they gave and how they formed, between the fox-trot that needed 40 yards to do the basic steps and the rhythmic, spine-jarring jerks of the samba, our characters to face the soot and sulphur of a typical steel-grey Edinburgh commercial or professional day.

There was also the New Cavendish Ballroom at Tollcross that seemed to include democratically working and middle classes and in which the dancers seemed to go through their motions with the absorbed dedication of priests and acolytes at some complicated ritual. It also had a night for the "over-30's"—poor, faded ghosts who, it was thought by heartless youngsters, were trying unsuccessfully to recapture their lost youth.

It was the Plaza, however, which saw me, primed with corrosive lemonade and strengthening chocolate biscuits, launch my first hesitant waltz and make my partner look at my feet and say: "Just give me a minute and I'll try and work out your steps." I'll never forget the exquisite agony of the moment. Farewell, old Plaza, I have only four words to say to you: "Slow, quick, quick, ouch."

35

To the Manor borne

IT is the country romance, legend, Border skirmishes, the lovingly-drawn setting for part of the action of a novel by John Buchan. Hare of the busy, night-trudging, body-snatching Burke partnership is believed to have had grave reservations about the place but did no free-lance excavation activities and worked there as an ill-paid labourer.

It is the haunt of the curlew whose lonely cry, evokes the spirit of the moorlands and soft rolling hills, the picknicker emitting the hoarse croak of car exhaust and transistor radio and, in any election, the elusive and transitory voter who may be at work in a farm, going about tasks of a useful domestic nature or out pacing the nearest field or peat bog, either in connection with some rustic activity or merely to stretch the legs in an area that has been described by Professor John Veitch in his *Border Essays* as "proportioned, restrained and complete as a Greek temple, supremely perfect and lovable" and with "a mysterious power of suggestion."

The place is the Manor Valley, two and a half miles south-west of Peebles, said by Sir Walter Scott to be "the sweetest vale of the South" and who drew inspiration from it for the first of the *Tales of My Landlord,* the home of David Ritchie, the so-called Black Dwarf whose gnarled features and misshapen body caused occasional female visitors to swoon and strong men to pale, and was yesterday the object of a visit by Mr Allan Macartney, Scottish National Party candidate for Tweeddale, Ettrick and Lauderdale, in his pursuit of bringing the message of democratic self-government for Scotland to the locals.

Buchan, in his stirring novel set in Stuart times which pulsates with the evocations of galloping horsemen, the clash and quiver of swordblades and dirty, dramatic and turbulent work amid the hills, forests and rivers of Peebleshire and surrounding Border areas, has a passage in which the hero arrives at Manor Water. "I stood still in wonder for there for the first time in my life I saw the stream dry. Manor, which is in winter a roaring torrent and at other times a clear, full stream, had not a drop of running water in its bed."

It was not so yesterday. The Manor Water, swollen to truculence by the recent rains, rippled its small, well-shaped muscles and flexed its perfectly-formed biceps. The surrounding hills wore scarves of misty chiffon in which blundered, depressed-looking sodden sheep, the fields and pasture lands were like giant sponges and the narrow road that snaked its way through the valley was flanked with passing places that had been transformed into shallow sheets of brown water occasionally raised to bow waves by passing cars.

Rainy canvassing in the painful electoral field does not daunt the dedicated and determined candidate and Mr Macartney, staff tutor in politics with the Open University in Scotland, writer, broadcaster and the party's Foreign Affairs' spokesman was not the aspirant to parliamentary status to flinch from showing a healthy brisket to the inclemencies of the weather.

"Take a lot of stickers in case we unearth massive support," he told his aides in Peebles with a smile, in which hope and stern canvassing experience were nicely blended, as they loaded the necessary electoral paper persuaders and sticky gestures of solidarity into their cars. They were ready for a safari into the valley that had known troubled times in the past—it had at least ten peel towers to repel the insolent English or feuding family foes—and was no doubt ready to deal with canvassers who penetrated its patchwork of hills, fields and scattered communities.

W.S. Crocket knew the valley. "There is an air of mystery surrounding it, and of old-worldly glamour that the mind can hardly rid itself of this feeling," he wrote in his *Scott Country*.

It was no doubt all there, the air, glamour, everything, but you had to look hard for it between overworked windscreen wipers. Around somewhere was Macbeth's Castle, a furtive structure that has apparently no connection with the Scottish monarch, well-known as a keen arborist, a farm that states with emphatic authority that no eggs are for sale to the public and an entrepreneurial cottage industry specialising in the free-lance sale of goat's milk.

The pioneering cars bumped and splashed their way on the rising, rough, rivulet-streaked road to the head of the valley—objective Manorhead Farm in the shadow and shelter of Dollar Law where 1,000 sheep feed on best-quality Scottish turf, a sight to gladden the eyes and heart and swell the hopes of any SNP candidate.

Across the mud and stones walked Mr Macartney dressed in smart blue jacket, matching trousers, large of rosette and smile and outstretched of hand. Mr Leslie P. Coltherd, who works the farm, sagged with rustic amazement at the sight of candidate, aides and Press. "Man, you must be keen to come up here," he said, pressing an iron, admiring hand into that of Mr Macartney. Mr Coltherd's son, Graham, working on the construction of a diesel fuel tank also seemed stricken with disbelief. If the black dwarf himself had lurched up to ask him his opinion about the Common Market agricultural policy and its effect on the price of black polled bullocks, he could have not been more surprised.

Mr Coltherd listened to what the candidate eloquently and quietly said about his party's policies, stared at his own large rubber boots, essential adjuncts to the agricultural life and said: "You're on a sticky wicket here." That was true enough since Mr Macartney seemed to be sinking into about six inches of mud.

Mr Macartney then put it straight from the interrogative shoulder. "Are you going to vote for me?" he asked. "No" said the honest elector, just like that. Oh the agony of the scene. The public little knows the sword-thrusts—as in a Buchan novel—that a candidate can get, and after a further inconclusive talk with Mrs Coltherd, the cars retreated down the bumpy road, mud-flecked and groaning at the springs.

Some of the houses in the area seemed deserted, as if the inhabitants had fled in terror from the menace of a General Election but as we drove along—I conveyed with safe passage by the candidate—we encountered Mr James Smellie, an elderly man who had farmed in the area for 30 years. "Going to vote Conservative," he told us. "Done so all my life and have no reason to change now."

Mr Macartney, swallowed hard and let him have a few words about what he thought of Conservative policies, especially in regard to Scotland's welfare. Mr Smellie seemed unimpressed but cordially wished the candidate good-luck and we drove off and halted in the Castlehill area at a settlement called Hillcrest. It was opened by a woman with a pleasant smile who stated emphatically that she would not be voting for the candidate. Mr Macartney steeled himself and prepared for the worst. He got it. Her vote she said firmly would go to the Liberal Alliance. The passion for truth among the inhabitants of the valley was getting to be dispiriting but Mr Macartney seemed unaffected.

The cars left the valley in faint sunshine but already the mists were closing in again and the air of mystery as to whether there might be an SNP voter about deepened. Time pressed, other places, no doubt, with their own triumphs and defeats, and Mr Macartney bravely gathered his electoral sling shots and left the enchanted valley to brood on its own business.

36

Moneypenny's revenge

ACCORDING to a newspaper report, Lois Maxwell, the 55-year-old actress who has played Miss Moneypenny—"M's secretary and secret idoliser of James Bond"—is to be replaced by a younger woman for Sean Connery's Bond comeback film *Never Say Never Again.* She is reported to be "furious."

These were stirring times in Room 412 of the 00 Section of the British Secret (in a manner of speaking) Service. Miss Moneypenny was making cocoa, not just for herself but for M, her boss, who had just told her that morning as gently as he could—his fine old espionage-pained eyes softening as he did so and the pulse in his forehead beating strangely—that orders had come from "above" that she was to be moved from her present post to a private secretaryship in an important—perhaps vital—section dealing with white fish landlings in West Highland ports.

"No reflection on your competency Miss Moneypenny," said M, giving one of his brief smiles—likened to the cold glint of dawn on a coffin lid—that lit up his eyes more than his mouth and his mouth more than his ears, "but times are changing, new brooms are sweeping and cupboard skeletons rattling as a result of all the latest spy revelations in Britain and our blessed leaderene—as I believe she is called—wants not just a complete shuffle among our pack of cards but the replacement of most of the cards themselves.

"I am being turfed out in favour of V, who in turn is being replaced by Z (pronouned in deference to our American

169

allies 'zee'). D is being moved up to replace him and you know what that will mean in promotional prospects for young C. Bond is to keep his job despite now having to use surgical stockings, deaf-aid, double-fixative for his wig and bifocal contact lenses but even he could be on the way for the ormulo presentation clock with the Walther PPK 9mm Kurz automatic action in the alarm, the golden flak jacket and the box of chocolate liqueur self-destruct pills."

Suddenly, the door creaked open and in lurched Bond carrying a regulation MI5 walking-stick with the emergency cough linctus in the handle, certain small, squat, but highly effective torpedo-shaped objects in the stem and the ephedrine inhaler at the other end.

He flung his tried and trusty, cough-expectorant-stained Trilby at the hat-stand, missed, hobbled over to pick it up, groaned arthritically as he did so, then made for Miss Moneypenny's desk with a low chuckle that sounded like British-made tonic wine being poured into a plastic glass.

He attempted ineptly to put an arm round the secretary but drew back hastily as her spine stiffened like a Pomeranian Grenadier on parade before a Kaiser. He then uttered a dry cough, the sound of which had once made men turn pale and run screaming to another chapter, and with his new false teeth clicking romantically, wheezed: "You're still a heart-throb Moneypenny. Some day you and I . . ." he broke off and shrugged as a fibrostic twinge got him in the lower left shoulder. Somewhere about him a varicose vein itched menacingly.

Miss Moneypenny's heart, strengthened by so much pointless throbing in the past, was still capable of missing a beat or two at the sight of James as well as at the sound of his voice, a curious mixture of consonantal pure Fettes,

Hollywood twang, rich Edinburgh Fountainbridge demotic and with just a hint of sensuous nasal catarrh.

There was only one thing she could say and she said it, straight, woman-like and from an elegantly-shaped shoulder: "Cocoa?" she asked huskily, her hazel eyes glinting with a strange fire like distant brake lights. Bond, a man who had once scorned the finest Tokay because it had been poured in a suspicious manner with the bottle pointing to the west instead of south-south-east and had been known to freeze an inferior Moulton Rothschild of Piesporter Goldropchen back into the decanter, grasped the Civil Service issue mug gratefully in his mittened fingers.

"Miss Moneypenny . . . I . . ." he said between robust Scottish sips. "James . . . you . . ." she prompted gratefully and hopefully. Just then M's voice crackled over the intercom. "Leave off Bond," it said. "At your age . . . you can come in now," and Bond, ever obedient to the asthmatic wheeze of duty, staggered away.

Miss Moneypenny clutched her Royal Wedding commemoration mug until her knuckles showed white under the strain. The story of her life in the quintessence of nutshell; one minute about to get her man with pension, insurances, old videotapes of *South Pacific* included and the next left standing among the carbon-paper, Prittsticks, paper clips and memoranda about the economic use of paper clips and warnings not to use office phones for finding out today's recipes and the cricket scores and with the steam of a discarded cup of cocoa, among other things, misting up her spectacles strangely.

She stuck a fag in the corner of her regulation cupid-bow, secretarial-type lips and groped for her lighter. Unable to find it, she folded a spare copy of document A/59/South

Atlantic/5C headed: "British Fleet Dispositions—1982 Falkland Islands" and shoved it into the gas fire. It burst into a gratifying flame and with it she lit up.

As the evocative wreaths swirled up to the smoke-stained ceiling, she reflected on her past life, largely misspent in breaking her fingernails over typewriters and her heart over James.

Once—was it the spring of 1962?—James had blown a kiss in her direction, an action that brought the glow of happy story endings to her eyes and improved the action of her skin. "James ... I ... you ..." she said, as he was rushed off on some assignment. He paused for just a second, shrugged his shoulders provocatively, smiled that exciting smile like a dog-leg slit trench, said: "You ... I ..." and was gone to chapter two with who knew what soft, slinky, seductive sirens.

She vaguely remembered the girls—hussies she would call them—who could never have been brought back by James to his mother, let alone Calvinistic M, and who could not be imagined knitting sweaters for James and videotaping the Delia Smith cookery course.

Lighting another cigarette with a copy of "Proposed Cruise Missile Sites—Cherbourg Peninsula, 1981," she reflected that she would have been so much better for him, a steadying influence, a solid British shoulder for him to lean on when the going got tough with Korean odd job men, female members of the Russian secret service and a certain Baltic citizen forever intent on bisecting Bond with a well-directed laser beam.

She could see James in her suburban heaven, perhaps named Spion Kop after a certain battle for the Empire, his finely-chiselled features frowning expertly as he tamed the snarling automatic drill to fit up new shelves and the way his "Don't shout at me, I've had a hard day" apron would fit so becomingly round his waist as he washed up.

She sighed and took a cocoa tin from a shelf. In it she put a folded copy of a document headed: "Drainage Plans for Merthyr Tydfil, Motherwell and Manchester: Top Secret." It nested cosily between documents headed "Boy Scout dispositions in Cumbria in the event of war," "Distribution of tent mallets: British Army," and "Present state of officers' trouser-pressers and hostilities-only supply plans."

Number 007 left with a blood-shot wink and a murmured: "Gosh . . . I . . . you," and she replied, almost mechanically in the same vein, her dream of bonding with James shattered like the dreams of Dr Who, Goldfinger, Smersh, Spectre, etc.

Into her capacious handbag she popped the cocoa tin and in her prim, spinster-type home, she picked up a phone. A heavily-accented Slavonic voice replied. It was that of X— the well-known heavy transport and fine art attache of the Russian Embassy. "Yuri: I've got the tin," she gasped passionately.

"You . . . I," he replied, his voice choking with emotional espionage and with a hint of relief in his manly voice. "I . . . you," she replied and she meant it. Her deed was no doubt dreadful but in a country leaking secrets like an old barge, she felt it hardly mattered if a few more went. In this world, a girl needed a little appreciation at some time in her life.

37

Cold comfort

ACCORDING to reports reaching me from several medical sources, an end to the common cold is in sight and that research workers at the Common Cold Research Laboratory in Salisbury are expecting successful results with the drug Interferon.

The news has sent a shiver of psychosomatic apprehension through British hypochondriac circles and resulted in a thoughtful leader in the monthly magazine *Hypochondria Today,* to which I am an enthusiastic subscriber.

An extract states: "Any move to eliminate the traditional native cold will be regarded by most, if not all, practising hypochondriacs as a move akin to destroying some age-old and revered structure like Stonehenge.

"Britain would not be Britain without its typical natives going about their work, red-nosed, eye-watering and plying their handkerchiefs vigorously. It is the British cold that has formed our character to stand up to adversity, made us battle into work despite the fact that we were trailing a wake of germs, using up packets of paper handkerchiefs and infecting our colleagues and it is the British cold that has done much to stimulate the growth of the pharmaceutical industry as well as helping to create and maintain the prosperity of chemist shops.

"We say that those who have colds and, more important in our view, those who think they have colds, should be allowed to enjoy their affliction in peace without the interference of bureaucrats and scientists forever dabbling

174

in fields where they have no business to be."

I hope the research workers in Salisbury, sniffing around cold bacilli and dropping them into volunteers, read that, especially Dr John Willman, clinical administrator at the laboratory who has stated that he is fairly confident that within five years they will be able to prevent people catching cold and certain common types of influenza. He hoped that by that time they would have developed the technique sufficiently of the use of Interferon to enable most people to be immunised against catching the cold.

The elimination of the common, not to say vulgar cold, could make the lives of millions of people in Britain, invalid. I would feel strangely uneasy, like a traveller in an alien land, in a future that did not have the common cold to enable me to try the latest Penicillin derivative supplied by my ever-generous doctor, give me a subject to talk about to people in buses, streets and in the office, and to present, with its regular incursions into my body, a kind of reassuring continuum of affliction coming and going like the slow swing of the seasons.

My normal state—and that of I imagine, many other people in Britain—is to have a cold, perhaps not what is graphically described as a "streaming" one, but a small, modest, even coy one, barely more than a sniffle and occasional handkerchief dip.

When I go out in the morning I take my cold with me for a light airing, the way people take their dogs. Like a dog owner, I share a common conversational bond with others so accompanied. On some wind-swept city links I will perhaps meet some other cold-carrying citizen and often we will exchange views about our faithful afflictions.

"Gosh, you're a fine, vigorous one," I will remark to some

citizen, patting his nose with his handkerchief as if the organ had taken first in the novice class at the Birmingham open cold show. "Yes," he might say in a self-congratulatory way, "brought it up from a mere snuffle when nobody though it would survive, fed it on anti-nasal drops, diet of mixed decongestants and it never has a day without a really good tablespoonful of marrowbone-enriched cough linctus. The result is as you see it, a credit to me and the British pharmaceutical industry. You seem to have a good, healthy one as well."

I too, will nod, perhaps a bit smugly because I am proud of my cold with its penetrating bark, the way my nose runs when the playful mood takes it and the way it goes everywhere with me, wakening me up in the morning and even—well, it's the nature of a cold, you can't blame it— trying to get into bed with me at night.

"Yes, it's not a bad one," I will say, sniffing at the far-off, germ-laden horizon with the action of a pointer dog. "I like to keep it fit by giving it nothing but the best multi-vitamin tablets, for a treat maybe a bit of night balsam to sniff at, and for exercise taking it continually from a warm atmosphere into a chilly one, and vice-versa. If you want a cold that will be your constant companion come winter rain or sleet or summer day, you have to give it continual attention and it will repay you in the long run."

If I look back on my psychosomatic life with its golden, youthful days of blowing into handkerchiefs in class, getting my first invigorating chest rub as a child and going my errant juvenile ways smelling richly of camphor, which threw a germ-deterrent and human-repellent screen around me, I realise that I have spent most of my days having a cold, recovering from one or about to start one.

You are never alone with a cold. Even if you are at home by yourself, a cold is a constant companion, taking your mind off other worries. It does not ask for much beyond perhaps a few capsules or pills from the chemist and the odd doctor's prescription. It is easily satisfied with a walk in the rain and high winds and if your shoes let in the wet, the cold will be eternally grateful to you and show it.

The *British Hypochondriac's Diary* this year is full of sage advice for the careful grooming of a cold, how to get it into really good physical shape so that it will still be as active in the summer as it is now, and some interesting facts on cold injections, that is, injections that will give you a fine, frisky cold rather than preventing you from having one.

With that are some rather engaging pictures of cold germs, apparently enjoying a joke in a typical human larynx taken at F11, 1/500, late summer.

There is also a highly informative article entitled: "Can you afford a cold?" about the iniquitously-high cost of pharmaceuticals and "Enjoying colds after 80," a neat little article about the cheerful people perhaps coming near to the end of life's cough bottle, who still maintain fine, full-bodied colds and would not thank you for any other affliction.

All that shows that in Britain today colds are a vital part of our way of life, the ending of which would be a big blow and cause cries of anguish and rage and the despairing waving of millions of unused paper handkerchiefs.

To what would people have left to turn if deprived of their colds—erysipelas? trench feet? dengue fever? The prospect is bleak indeed.

I have only two words to say to those scientists seeking to deprive us of our natural birth-right of colds and allied afflictions and who probe into our private ills with the sinister Interferon. One is "Aaah," and the other, as you might readily guess, is "Choo," and to Dr Willman especially, I mean them to sting.

38

A song in the windy night

WHEN you get to my incredibly antique age—
35½ if a night—and live in one city for most of
your life you build up a large compost-heap of
memories which a walk through scenes of childhood,
adolescence and early manhood will instantly set ablaze in
the spontaneous combustion of recall.

Here for instance, at that street corner, I thought the
thoughts of youth, though what they were has now escaped
me. About here, I fought the fights of youth over matters
which are equally elusive. There, by that shop—no, not the
Chinese carry-out one called Wan Sik Tum but the one
which says it specialises in cooked meat products of all
types—I was, at the age of ten, accosted one evening by an
eight-year-old girl, name of Elma, and asked who was my
sweetheart. When, in a moment of sudden and tactful
inspiration, I indicated that she was, she seemed touched
and gratified and never raised the matter again.

It was around a lamp-post which partially lit up a dark
corner between two houses and was of the old, green-
painted, gas type, that I and a school friend, John, spent
many of the golden hours of our childhood.

Under the Arctic blue stars of winter or in the crisp spring
evenings when the air was like wine and the malt bouquet
from the many breweries hung over the city like a benison
and to take a good deep breath could make one's head spin
with mild alcoholic shock, John, who knew wrestling grips,
having watched the Homeric struggles between his mother

179

and father over domestic matters, passed on his esoteric knowledge to me. For hours we used to grunt and sweat like rival stags, arms, hands and legs locked in combat and when our parents tried to separate us, they almost had to use crowbars.

Then one night, to our chagrin, we found our pitch had been taken by a female, well-stricken in years, aged, I suppose, about 30.

Her somewhat battered bonnet gave encouraging promise of other signs of eccentricity, richly borne out by her action of suddenly singing hymns and psalms to the empty urban spaces and speaking on the need for morality in life. On her delicate features she had, to the delight of two juvenile barbarians, a moustache which wriggled on her moving upper lip like a restless insect.

She came to the spot about twice a week, her tiny orb of song often whirled away in the rude, masculine gusts of a windy city night. John and I were generally the only audience she had. She believed, I think, that we were angelic but we were only watching her upper lip for a new convulsion.

Sometimes we questioned her closely on certain theological matters. "God is love," she told us. "Why?" we asked. In ready answer she produced for us a couple of calendars with painted angels on them and a three-word message which confirmed her statement.

Eventually even her attractions palled and we left for other juvenile pastimes. Sometimes on a wet and blustery night we could hear her singing bravely, her bonnet askew and her message falling on the deaf, dark city streets.

The other night I walked along the street and saw that the spot on which the lamp-post stood had been built over.

Sullen youths slouched in shadows and the graffiti on the walls seemed like the slime of some foul passing slug. The wind whistled in the alleyways and suddenly in it, for me, the message came thin but clear: "God is love: God is love."

She has gone from the streets but here's a funny thing. I haven't forgotten her and I know I never shall.

39

A show of cards

I saw an advertisement in a newspaper the other day which stated: "Salesman wanted for well-known pharmaceutical firm. Must be enterprising, hard-working, self-starting. Generous salary, holidays, expenses, bonuses, etc. Occasional foreign travel, excellent canteen facilities. Perks include office card."

The last-mentioned item interested me strangely. An office card? Something, I may say, that in the early days of my journalistic career I coveted, the possession of which to me signified status in a way that not even a rolled-up black brolly and bowler hat—two essential pieces of equipment for reporters in the old days—would have done.

I used to stand on some occasions among a group of reporters on an assignment, perhaps waiting to interview some dignitary, and it used to sear my sensitive soul to see some gentlemen of the English Press go up to the interviewee and hand him cards which might say: "Jeremy Sign of the *Times*" or "Fred Stir of *The Bugle*."

The dignitary would nod affably as he recognised the names that graced the illustrious columns of those papers and he would unship some required comments to the card-carriers. Sometimes, he would take out his own card and hand it to them, the action resembling that of warships at sea exchanging salutes by raising and lowering flags or firing blank shots from cannon.

The rest of us who had no cards hung around grieving silently at the omission of our office management to supply us with such vital news-gathering adjuncts. After writing the comments in our notebooks, we left feeling inferior and as journalist hewers of blunt, uncouth, sentences and unworthy drawers of salaries.

In my most secret journalistic dreams I used to see myself with a card of my very own, new or having been possessed only by one careful previous owner, with his name scored out and mine written in or printed over. I did not ask for much, something say three inches long by one and a half inches wide that would show the world that I had arrived significantly on the newspaper scene. "Albert Morris— writer, " it would say, just like that, and in smaller letters it would give the name and address of the paper that had the honour and expense of employing me.

It never happened and I can now reveal that some of the worst psychological scars I received during my career as a newsman came from being deprived of an office card.

I would, at the end of some interview, prepare to leave. The person from whom I had been dredging facts would say: "Please give me your name and address in case I have anything further to say to you. Perhaps you could let me have your card."

I would then shamefacedly have to confess that I did not have one either had to write the required information on a piece of scrap paper or else would use a suitably torn cigarette packet for the purpose.

The interviewee would watch me with some pity as I went through that undignified ritual. He would then say: "Here is my card in case you want to contact me again," and leave as I haemorrhaged with chagrin and embarrassment and wished that my paper was somewhat less mean with cardboard.

As the steeling years came and went, I found that many people I had been at school with were in possession of office cards which they flaunted before me and which bore statements like: "Harold Grasper, managing director, Butterlove Brothers, export and import consultants." or "Miss Cynthia Pindrop, personnel manager, Girning & Co."

"You haven't got a card Albert?" they would say as I cringed from their ill-concealed scorn. It was like having to confess that I did not have a colour television set with remote-control switch, central heating, double-glazing and a key to the office executive toilet suite.

"Take mine," many would say in sudden bursts of generosity and soon my wallet would begin to bulge with the cardboard indicators of the office success of people who, when they were in class with me and such cards were only distant goals on a far commercial horizon, could hardly parse a sentence, solve a quadratic equation or realise that the square on the hypotenuse of a right-angled triangle was equal to the sum of the squares on the other two sides.

Never mind. I would comfort myself with the knowledge that office cards were not everything in life and when the card-givers left me, no doubt to get more supplies for their wallets or handbags, I would tear up their offerings and drop them as a small but revengeful blizzard into the wastepaper basket.

I am glad I did not live in the days when the middle-class upwards were always leaving calling cards in people's houses and expecting invitations for social occasions on the strength of such actions. I would probably not have graduated to the social strata that flourished such oblong indications of correct behaviour and would have been, I suspect, just under the card-carrying classes and going about my business clutching my cloth cap in frustration and thinking that perhaps that Marx chap, who envisaged a brave, new, cardless world, had a lot more in his writings than many people imagined.

I do, as a matter of necessity, carry some cards. My trade union one has my signature on it and a photograph that shows me glaring into space as if about to pass a resolution to suspend standing orders. I also have various credit and shopping account cards but in the space of my wallet marked "office card," there exists only a humiliating emptiness.

The other day I saw a colleague open a packet of personal office cards and shove some into his wallet. "Where," I asked aghast and because I wanted to know, "did you get them?"

He revealed that this paper supplied them to writers of note and that if qualified for that description I, even I, might have a gross or two to flip across to admiring readers who might be short of material to light a fire or jam a rattling window.

Inquiries revealed that he was in all respects correct and that I only had to indent to have my office packed from sentence to sentence with my very own cards stating: "Albert Morris, columnist and inspirational writer. Assuring you of my best attention at all times."

I had to admit that I felt felled as if by a sandbag. At first a glorious sense of expectation came on me but was quickly followed by one of dejection. It was like a man who sees the girl of his dreams for the first time and suddenly realises that she is 16 and he is 85.

"To late," I groaned. I had become used to being without cards and the thought of such printed riches being showered on me was just too much for my wallet—not used to bearing great weights—to take. Perhaps I had even become card bored.

Suddenly, the clink of glasses made me realise that Miss Angela Primstone, chatelaine of the columnar wine cupboard was bearing down on me silently, as if on castors, with a glass of rare old Moldavian tokay, once the property of the late King Ferdinand of Bulgaria. "What advantage could a card be to a gentleman the likes of you," she whispered consolingly in my left, or good ear. Cardless, I may be, but as I sipped a glass with the lady and ate a slice of claret-enriched, Edinburgh seed-cake, I realised that there were compensations.

40

Rising tide of verbiage

I was sitting at my desk the other day brooding on the inscrutable workings of fate—as no doubt Lord Carrington and Mrs Thatcher were also doing at the time—when Mr J.C. Feeney, chief typographical error overlooker, rushed into my office, his face working strangely as if under the grip of great emotion.

With hardly a pause to touch what was left of his forelock, he gasped: "There's trouble at No. 3 shaft in the giant verbiage refining and distribution plant. One of the vats has burst its sides because of a sudden surge of pressure from Government pamphlets and local authority circulars and has flooded the verb de-activating department, the pleonasm-finishing shop, the phrase-turning assembly and the prose-purpling spray area.

"There's men trapped down there, maybe women too. I've done everything I can. I . . ." and here the great columnar artisan swayed as if in the grip of a faint and was revived only by a quick draught of Imperial Hungarian Tokay taken straight from the columnar wine cupboard by a prompt Miss Angela Primstone, chatelaine of that important, perhaps vital, dusty, cob-web-lined, odoriferous closet.

To think with me is but to act and realising as columnar squire, responsibilities with full powers to act, I rushed down the narrow spiral stairways to the scene of the accident and there saw a sight which, though not perhaps as terrifying as the results of the well-known dambursting raids of

Germany during the last hostilities in Europe, was spectacular enough to make even me catch my breath and wonder— but for a moment only—what should be done.

A massive roaring cataract of turbulent, white-margined verbiage was pouring unrestrictedly from the outlet shaft into the vital heart of the columnar assembly area, hissing as it touched white-hot inspirational ingots due to be slotted and welded without a seam into paragraphs, gurgling as it surged into the laboratory area, destroying carefully cultivated germs of ideas and murmuring in a replete sort of way as it scooped up *en passant* examples of untreated litotes, low-grade oxymoron and crude meilosis all due to be shovelled into the great columnar processing plant and to appear later, sparking or gleaming in carefully structured sentences with superbly tooled verbs, high quality nominative and adverbial clauses and precision-made adjectives of unparalleled descriptive powers.

A groan, low at first, but rising in volume, came from behind the deluge. An apprentice from the sentence-parsing and infinitive splitters' machine room clutched at my elbow with a grimy, adjective stained hand, pointed a quivering finger at the flood and cried hoarsely: "It's them in the main conjunction stripping shop. There's 53 people trapped. One of them," he added with simple artisanal dignity, "is my brother."

There was only one thing to do and I did it. Pausing only to divert myself of my columnar hat, jacket and waistcoat, I decided that the only way to reach the vat and turn off the stopcocks was up No. 3 shaft itself.

"Don't!" shrilled Miss Primstone. "Let me go instead. The world will not miss me." Pausing again but only to commend her for willingness to place herself in possible danger, I pushed her aside with a brisk but manly gesture and plunged into the maelstrom of paper.

It was hard going. My initial plunge had dislodged a massive collection of Government pamphlets and, as Forestry Commission annual report and account, arboricultural leaflets and grey squirrel control notices floated past me. I ran up against mortality statistics for 1980-81 and the Euphorbiacoae of New Guinea—two ugly, jagged pieces that nearly had me pinned to the side of the shaft and pulled under.

It was dark in the shaft, cold too. I thought a lot about my past life in there as I struggled gasping against the tide, how I had started off as a mere journalistic stripling with little more to read than some simple civil aviation amendment bill or an interim report on archaeological sites in South-west North Uist, maybe a hand-out on pest control in Sutherlandshire or yet another free gift offer from Readers' Digest or some altruistic book club.

It was easy then but as the years went on my youthful acne carriage became bent under the weight of words that I had to carry for professionalism's sake. Local authority hand-outs, public relation firms' outpourings, income-tax leaflets and forms, the growing bulk of words from the Automobile Association, the near-lethal weight of opinions from the quality Sunday papers, the public library books piled up to be read, the volumes bought new or second-hand from book-shops which I will probably never open this side of judgment day and probably not even after, all piled up around me to make my life at times a reading hell.

Suddenly, out of the darkness came the awful roar of Department of Environment official guides. Here was a grim, jagged one entitled "Edinburgh Castle—32 pages,

£0.80p" and another, granite hard with facts called "Tantallon Castle—eight pages of plates and diagrams, £0.85p." With one bound I pulled myself against a stanchion, dodged them as well as "Standard specification for water and sewerage schemes," and battled on.

Was there no end to it all? Two towering pamphlets dealing with reductions in the rates' support grant had me under for several seconds but I managed to surface spluttering and striking out strongly in order to dodge one from St Andrew's House on housing capital allocation and several letters from some friendly computer offering me the benefit of a private health scheme and reduced car insurance premiums for the over-sixties.

As my stomach was giving out, and I was only just managing to brush aside a document on incineration in molten sacks of alpha-contaminated solid waste. I reached the end of the shaft, staggering up to the vat which showed signs of collapsing under the weight of words, turned off the supply of verbiage to it with about the same effort as one would make to close the floodgates of some dam, then waited, tired but triumphant, for the flood to subside.

Eventually the trapped workers were able to emerge and for some reason. I was hoisted on their shoulders and eventually tossed into the air to the accompaniment of huzzas.

It was nothing, of course, as I mentioned quietly to them but Miss Primrose gazed at me with what I thought was something more than hero-worship in her hazel eyes in which strange shadows played.

I read somewhere that many local authorities in Britain have complained about being almost submerged by floods of verbiage sent to them that have gone beyond previous record flood levels and that emergency clearing operations had to be planned to prevent possible danger to the mind and bodies of staff, much of the surplus matter being diverted, I understand, to engulf other individuals and organisations.

Perhaps people reading this will realise the growing dangers of life in this over-papered civilisation of ours. As usual, I am only trying to help.

41

A Hulot holiday

A S I sit by my electric imitation-log fire watching the
ever-recurring pictures in the flames and surrounded
by the first crop of holiday brochures for next year
that have dropped with a leaden premonitory thud through
my letter box, my mind drifts willingly away from the study
of garish Mediterranean and West Indian beaches, azure
skies flecked with palms and the bold angularities of luxury
hotels and of pictures of fishing boats dotted photogenically
along some languid littoral.

It goes through labrynthine passages of memory to
emerge in the sunlight of some half-remembered Eden to
that idyllic vacation taken by M. Hulot in Brittany so many
years ago when a video tape recorder for household use was
only a dim dream in some scientist's mind, British stamps
still tended to present the austere face of the monarch to the
world and little else and there were still many places on this
Earth where you could have a quiet holiday in a seaside
hotel away from the sound of all-night discos, the roar of
passing traffic, guests, probably British, tearing the establishment apart with bare hands and minds and where the
dining tables were still free of convenience food and bread
that tasted like the product of some plastics' plant.

When he made *M. Hulot's Holiday* in 1951, Jacques Tati
who died last week aged 73, presented an acutely-observed,
delicately-humoured and eccentric tale of a vacation in a
quiet, holiday resort set amid the cliffs of Brittany. Apart
from the inspired comedy of that essentially gentle film that

192

affectionately recorded the idiosyncrasies and behavioural convulsions of the human race away from its natural domestic or work habitat, the film was memorable for me in presenting the kind of holiday I have always sought and never quite managed to achieve.

The days were characterised by almost perpetual sunshine that bathed the small, sand-flecked resort in the kind of refulgent light that made for feelings of well-being relaxed attitudes and the generally shared desire among holiday makers to address each other by way of polite nods or a few, barely heard observations about the clemency of the weather.

What always strikes me about that superb film is its quietness and its impressionistic image of a dream-world in which the gentle sea-wind sighs softly among the sand dunes, the little waves curtsy in small white skirts and retreat with a faint modest swish and the sky is clear of any clouds indicating sudden meteorological change and resulting in days spent in the hotel lounge staring at the rain-drops zig-zagging down window panes or in reading old magazines.

In that film there were hardly any sentences strung together that seemed to make sense; all was half-heard, suggested with upraised eyebrows, perhaps downcast lips or with an eloquent gesture of hand, head or shoulders.

The hotel itself appeared as a distinct personality with its perpetually squeaky doors, its elegant wooden structure that seemed as weathered as a sun-and-sea-scoured beach tree-trunk and with its waiters regarding some of the idiosyncratic guests with barely concealed expressions of disbelief or wonder.

The beach seemed, compared with today's thronged

sand-traps for sunbathers, almost empty of people and those who did frequent it had a kind of somnambulistic appearance as if the magical quietness of the place had entered into their souls and put them into a kind of waking dream of warm sand and soft breezes and where each day was like a benison.

The guests, even those of charmingly-odd character like M. Hulot himself, were unfailingly well-mannered and no doubt went to their rooms at a respectably early hour without feeling the need to dance until dawn, shout or sing in the corridors or fling chairs into the swimming pool, although in this case the hotel did not have the refinement of such a pool, the management perhaps believing that the waves which were good enough to bear the ship that carried the beauteous Iseult to Tristram, were good enough for the sportif bodies of its guests.

The resort itself also seemed wrapped in the atmosphere and texture of a dream, its buildings appearing almost as if they had somehow risen from the ground by supernatural upheaval to take their place among the superbly-sculptured cliff scenery and they also had a look of impermanence as if they might blow away at a sudden and extra-strong puff of wind.

But such a wind, of course, could not appear in that temperate of climes which seemed like the magic valley of Avalon to which the stricken Arthur was taken by his queens on a black barge borne on rolling and pitching Tennysonian verse. As in a few of the Tati films there is always the girl—more of a sprite really than a creature of real life—shy, pretty but not startlingly so, with frank, smiling eyes, a kindly mouth and with a sense of humour that corresponds so exactly to the kind of girl the lone male could meet on a holiday romance. They would leave with mutual expressions of regret and promises to write to each other and meet again if they could. In the Hulot stories, one knew that they never would meet again and that their encounter would be the stuff of faded holiday snaps, vague memories, puzzled frowns and attempts to remember the name of the other.

What, one wonders, would that hotel be like now? I suspect it would have been completely rebuilt so that it would resemble a concrete, glass and plastic fortress and have accommodation for about 600 guests in rooms complete with private bath, colour TV, radio and balcony.

The guests would not come in single spies but in battalions, processed and packaged like factory products, arriving in bus-loads and sent away in the same manner to make room for the next consignment to arrive.

The beach would be crammed with people equipped with the latest lotions for enhancing or speeding-up the bronzing of the skin, transistor radios that will cracklingly blare rock music, innumerable children and adults kicking footballs, shops offering souvenirs and food and the sea will be flecked with sailing dinghies, water-skiers and motor-craft, the latter causing white weals on the sea in their whining wake.

At night, the hotel would reverberate to some over-amplified rock group in the smoky, dark, hangar-like room given over to the spirit of dance and noise, and couples, like the middle-aged English one in the film, who spent much of the evening on the beach, the woman assiduously gathering shells and the man just as busily throwing them away, would seem as pale ghosts of a quieter and comparatively innocent past.

There would be no place for the M. Hulot who wanted to feel the great placidities of a vacation ease into his nervous system although there might be one for the character who created a kind of maniac chaos wherever he went.

Such a place as that resort, I suspect, has gone and will never return except in the holiday brochures of our dreams or in repeats of that supremely-funny and oddly-wistful work. Thank you, M. Tati, for the film; to me it was almost as good as a good holiday to see it.

42

Missing the buskers

AMONG the many inspiriting and inspiring experiences of my life resulting from hearing, say, some revelational theme of a great symphony, a fragment of verse that drew me to a faery lands forlorn seen through metrical magic casements, the miracle of composition and purity of line of some painting or a passage from the Bible and Shakespeare that revealed some deep truth about the nature of the human spirit, seeing a one-man band perform in Edinburgh one murky night of rain, hail, sleet and a wind that fell on the face like the rasp of a rusty razor, ranks as one of the greatest.

Amid the sound of clattering chimney cans and the sight of flying hats, out-turned umbrellas, fluttering skirts and the wares of newsvendors flying like a blizzard, I saw and marvelled at this lone performer of the night.

His features were covered with the tragi-comical mask of the clown. He had on a white shirt, red jacket and wide-striped, baggy trousers but it was the sheer, exuberant ingenuity of his performance that utilised just about every movable part of the human frame, which commanded instant attention from those not pinned against walls or sucked up one street and blown down another by the wind.

With one hand he beat on a large drum strapped in front of him, with the other he tapped rythmically on a small side drum. At the sides of his knees were fastened cymbals which he clashed with explosive effect. His lips played a mouth-organ fixed on a frame round his neck. His nose operated a peremptory car horn mounted on the same frame and the back of his head was used to operate a kind of cushion which emitted spasmodic wailing sounds like a courting tom cat. I believe his ankles were fixed to small bells and—memory may play me false here—I think he did something useful with his ears and feet.

The sound he gave out on that dismal night was one of the most unusual I have heard, combining fair-ground musical cacophony, the beat of a triumphant army, a gaggle of wild geese passing, a pagan dance of joy for some strange god and just a hint of what the last trump would sound like.

The man's gyrations, his arms, legs, elbows and other parts of his body working in curious combination as well as the oddly rythmed sound his instruments produced, brought an instant uplift of the spirits. "Blow winds," as Lear said, "and crack your cheeks, rage, blow you cataracts and hurricanoes, spout till you have drenched our steeples, drown'd the cocks," but mankind, the performer seemed to say in a mixture of bangs, whistles, fragmented tunes, horn blasts and tinkles, was undismayed. Man, foolish, glorious, comical and impertinent would, if he had the power and notion, cock an unquenchably cheerful one-man band at the universe itself.

I don't know what possessed the fellow to perform on such a night but the box-office takings were predictably poor. After I had slipped a coin into a wet, grateful hand, he turned on his musical heels and marched off, playing defiantly in the direction of Edinburgh's purse-proud West End and I made my way through the sodden street feeling buoyed and bouncing as a yacht mooring.

That is what I expect of buskers, an injection of instant

and sometimes unexpected entertainment, although I admit few of them have come up to that impressive level of performance. Nevertheless, I am always glad to see these freebooters of the street theatre who do not seem to be as numerous in Edinburgh—except at time of Festival when most are obviously not local products—as they used to be when I spent my angel infancy and the golden hours of my youth waiting inordinately long times in queues for theatre and cinema.

Busking, as I know it, is a kind of spontaneous folk art which springs, if not from the soil, as least from the granite sett, the paving stone and gutter. For those waiting to get into a cinema or theatre it offers a kind of aperitif, hinting at greater entertainment glories to come, or suggesting that what one might see inside, no matter how expensive the seats, will not in any way equal the fluidity of movement, the sheer weight of talent for tearing up telephone books or making absorbing patterns from torn pieces of newspaper that one glimpses beside the dimly-lit entrance to the place of entertainment itself.

The buskers I have seen make in my memory a kind of Bayeux tapestry of jugglers, singers, tap dancers, horse-shoe straighteners and iron-bar-benders who took queuers' minds off the drill instructions of the bemedalled major-domos of commissionaires who ruled cinema-goers with iron voices and whose words like: "Four doubles at 2s 6d and five single at 1s 9d" seemed as authoritative as a pronouncement thundering from Mount Sinai.

There were, of course, buskers of extraordinary talent who could easily outshine many of the performers whose name appeared in capital letters on the posters outside the theatre. Others however made their money, less by the excellence of their technique than by practicing a kind of blackmail on their audiences.

One busker who used to set up his stage by the queues of Edinburgh's Playhouse cinema had a voice that sounded like a tortured cry from the rack of Torquemada's Inquisition. It belonged to an elderly gentleman who wore an old, greasy, cloth cap and a raincoat, the appearance of which resembled the interior of a smoke-begrimed railway tunnel.

To hear his voice singing' "Martha, Rambling Rose of the Wildwood," was to hear the authentic call of something barely human keening over old forgotten sorrows. It chilled the marrow, froze the blood and made the mind dwell on unpleasant web-footed creatures hopping about in a fetid, medieval dungeon.

People paid him money, not because they wanted to hear him, but because they wanted him to go away and take his voice, as well as the long, swirling, wake of flies that invariably came with him, away to some other cringing queue.

There were too the elderly ladies who lovingly kept winding ancient gramophones that played only one record, which sounded as if it was deep in some stormy ocean. They would appear at cinema queues the way vultures massed in the track of some army in the hope—vain in the ladies' case—of rich pickings for their cultural offerings.

I suppose some of the most joyous buskers I have seen were in London, especially the well-known one who with rolled-up trouser legs and collapsible umbrella performed hilarious tap-dance routines for audiences in the Haymarket, sometimes alone and sometimes with a female and whose double-jointed antics resembled those of that one-time music hall trio Wilson, Keppel and Betty.

I see from a report in this paper that Glasgow District Council's licensing committee are to set up a special committee to investigate the licensing of buskers to perform in the city streets.

I am with Mr Charles Horsburgh, the licensing committee clerk who warned that the committee would be ill-advised to control that sort of activity officially. He wondered how the committee could distinguish between the down-and-out with his mouth organ and buskers with obvious talent.

Exactly so. Busking, I believe is often a spontaneous, joyful activty giving pleasure to those who perform and those who see it and must not suffer from the dulling hand of bureaucracy.

Would that lone drum-thumper, mouth-organ-blower, cymbal-banger and horn-blaster have felt better if he had performed under the illustrious authority of Edinburgh's District Council? I doubt it. He was a creature of the elements, a manifestation of the free-lance, unfettered spirit giving his best in the worst of all possible worlds. My memory of that unlicensed performer is still undimmed and my thanks to him has not grown less in the passage of the jarring, clashing, years.

43

King Kong at 50

I am indebted to breakfast television for reminding me that last week saw the 50th birthday of that giant simian whose first appearance on the screens in 1933 made cinema audiences clutch their popcorn bags until their knuckles showed white under the strain and realise that there were more things in Hollywood's fevered commercial imagination that was dreamed of in their filmic philosophies.

Fifty eh? Now there is a time when a monster can pause for rest and reflection and consider not just his place in the script but his position in the universe and the inscrutable workings of fate.

At that respectable age, when the human species can still see the golden glow of youth on one side of its life and glimpse the darkening but not uninteresting landscape on the other, a monster such as the one that fancied Fay Wray—who could say why, a monster's thoughts are short thoughts and often the triggers for instant and dramatic action—must feel that the possibilities for youthful extravagancies and follies are lessening.

I have no doubt that King by now would have been experiencing a few twinges in the lower lumbar region, perhaps an ache or two in the joints when the barometric pressure fell significantly and more and more, a disinclination for earth moving and urban demolition to get the object of his heart's desire sitting on the upper heart line of his palm and certainly a fading ambition to shin up the Empire State Building and make largely ineffectual and physically exhausting passes at fighter planes buzzing around him with malevolent intent.

At 50, I believe, your average monster wants to take it easy for a bit, hit the hay rather than a passing subway train and spill out its passengers like peas from a pod, and to regard the latest female sacrifice with a mild interest that is quickly broken when her screams give him a persistent headache.

At 50 your average ape, I believe, would want to spend more time at home, perhaps taking a little light exercise by fending off the attention of a gigantic boa constrictor or a pterodactyl that, like a tropical insect, refused to be discouraged, and sit around with his peer group, assuming he had any, perhaps discussing the old days in Hollywood and the possibilities of getting a good agent to break into the world of commercial advertising.

If he had undertaken some simian arrangement that corresponded to marriage I suspect that the lady of the cave would be intimating to him that he was continually getting under her feet and asking why he was not stirring himself to go down to the native village and see what had been left for his as a non-burned offering.

He would probably heave up his vast bulk, unship a sigh that sounded like a wind tunnel at full sonic peak and shuffle down to the sacrifice stone probably telling himself that the sacrifices didn't taste the same these days—all that chemical feeding and soya bean substitute that the United Nations' relief funds supplied to the natives—and even spear points, bullets, arrows and burning stakes, lightly done, that were hurtled at him from time to time had somehow lost their flavour.

Not only that but he might have a distinct wheeze as he

walked. Nothing serious mind you that the slow balsam-type inhaling of the burning remains of a village he could wreck wouldn't cure but it would, with its sound of an elderly train panting up a steep gradient, warn the local population of his coming and thus the great element of surprise and visual shock would tend to be lost.

For a monster of that age, I suspect it is not much fun being expected to go about beating one's chest, roaring in the decibel equivalent of a squadron of dive-bombers, being expected to carry it off with some rag and bone and hank of hair that had been tied up for his delectation and to gratify the primitive and obstructive religious beliefs of a bunch of ethnic under-achievers who inhabited the same island as he did and which was badly in need of a good drainage expert and landscape gardener.

Even if one were taken to New York—the Elysium of monster capitalist exploitation—the scenario was not all that good and one could get mixed reactions from audiences, especially from people who had just woken up from a deep sleep and saw large ape orbs staring at them through windows. Crowd control was poor, street furnishings tended to come away in the hand and unless you had a head for heights you could get very bad Press notices.

I have always felt a great deal of sympathy for Kong, either as a young ape with big ideas or a middle-aged one, perhaps disillusioned by fickle fame and the fleeting nature of public interest. The females he became interested in were—as might be expected—totally unworthy of his mighty heart, instinctive grasp of gentlemanly courtesy and innocent though persistent romantic advances.

It was ever thus, I probably felt, as I saw him for the first time when I was but a lad of some five summers, the male,

an obvious Adam symbol, invariably let down by the
female who did not understand his simple, generous 24
carat heart and one carat mind.

When I first saw King Kong, the world was probably—
compared with what it is now—a more innocent place.
There was still some terra incognita about and the
possibility of a lost island or plateau where gigantic
creatures existed—perhaps left-overs from the age of
reptiles or sub-standard makes originally intended for
Eden—still seemed within the bounds of reality.

The Pacific island in which Kong stalked about moodily
causing a lot of condensation and extra cloud cover as a
result of his heavy breathing, was a superb creation from
the fevered Gothic imagination of Hollywood. My mind
swiftly grew captive to the fascinating and persistent gloom
of the place in which creatures of Jurassic age structure and
temper stalked about and which in its way was a kind of
reverse image of that other lost world planted for fully-
ribbed Adam somewhere in the Middle East.

The more sagacious members of cinema audiences, in
between shifting their old English humbugs from one cheek
to another, knew that Kong's end was bound to be tragic as
he was a kind of Hamlet, Othello and Romeo figure all
rolled into one bawling, breast-beating, affection-seeking,
hirsute mobile mountain.

Assuming that he is still alive and did not really perish
under US Air Force machine guns, let that lad at 50 rest,
stare at the pictures in the flames of villages he might have
absentmindedly obliterated and muse on a life that—
considering the gross commercial impulses of Hollywood—
might have been worse than it was.

He might have got Fay Wray permanently. Let a giant be
thankful for small mercies.